Women at Work:
Discrimination and Response

Stephen G. Peitchinis

M&S

Canadian Cataloguing in Publication Data
   Peitchinis, Stephen G., 1925-
      Women at work: discrimination and response

   Bibliography: p.
   ISBN 0-7710-6966-9

   1. Sex discrimination in employment – Canada. 2. Women –
   Employment – Effect of automation on – Canada. 3. Sexual division
   of labour – Canada. 4. Women – Employment – Canada. I. Title.
   HD6060.5.C2P44   1989   331.4'133'0971   C88-094581-8

Printed and bound in Canada

McClelland & Stewart Inc.
The Canadian Publishers
481 University Avenue
Toronto, Ontario
M5G 2E9

Contents

Tables and Figures

Figures

Acknowledgements

The writing of a book involves research, critical analysis, discussion, composition, and seemingly endless drafts. At each stage different people are commonly involved: research assistants, expert readers and discussants, willing and captive listeners, secretaries and typists. To all participants in the production of this small volume, I extend my gratitude. A special thank you to my wife, Dr. Jacquelyn Peitchinis, whose advocacy of equity in employment for women has been a life long activity, and whose frequent commentaries on the reality of women in the workplace provided the initial incentive to embark on this project. A special thank you also to Mrs. Judi Pearce, for her dilligence, efficiency, and patience in typing the manuscript through the many stages of production.

Stephen G. Peitchinis
The University of Calgary

Introduction

It is well that we begin with two anecdotes that manifest the social and cultural reality of the employment of women, a reality that has typecast women in society and the economy and that continues to be an imperfection to the efficient allocation and use of the services of women.

The first involves a little girl who sold lemonade to a group of golfers. She had set up a table next to the fifteenth green, which adjoined the backyard of her home, selling lemonade in very small plastic cups to thirsty and frustrated golfers at twenty-five cents per gulp, clearly taking advantage of the absence of competition and the high utility value of that gulp on a hot day. One of the golfers complimented the little girl and wondered aloud at what stage of their development do little girls lose the entrepreneurial spirit they demonstrate in childhood. He commented that little girls deliver newspapers, sell chocolate bars door-to-door, set up lemonade stands, do their own shopping, and are better students than boys. "Look at her," he said, "she is no more than about five years of age, yet she saw a potential market demand and established an enterprise to supply it. That is initiative."

The responses of his golfing partners are most instructive of prevailing social attitudes. To one of them the little girl's lemonade stand was a manifestation of domesticity, an innate desire to serve. The charge of twenty-five cents was incidental. She saw these thirsty, tired, frustrated men putting on the green, heard their not very nice comments about the ball not dropping into the cup, and her female instinct told her to provide that cooling antidote. To another golfer, the little girl's action must have been instigated by her mother, who wanted her out of the house while she played bridge, or was on the telephone or having tea with her neighbours. The fourth golfer pointed in the direction of the house, where a number of little boys were playing football, and said, "Initiative and entrepreneurship, my foot! They put her up to it. They probably got the idea, organized it, set up the stand, had their mother make the lemonade, hired the little girl to serve it, and they collect the profit. They are the entrepreneurs, and they are clearly enjoying it."

This perhaps demonstrates the perspectives of most adults (not only men, but women as well) toward boys and girls. Such perspectives socialize boys and girls into distinct groups and attribute to each different qualities and economic potentialities, as if founded on physiology and not on culture.

The second story concerns an automobile accident involving a father and his young son. The father is killed in the accident and the little boy is critically injured. The boy is rushed to the hospital and into the operating room. The surgeon looks at the boy and says, "I can't operate on him, he is my son." How is this possible? Was the father not killed in the accident? A stepfather perhaps? The puzzle is yet another manifestation of social conditioning founded on prevailing common practice. Surgeons have generally been men; and the word "surgeon" has come to have a male connotation. It is somewhat unusual to think of the surgeon as the boy's mother.

The attitudes manifested in these two stories constitute significant occupational and employment barriers for women. They are the sort of barriers that will not be found in job descriptions, and as such are not overtly exclusionary. Such barriers are subtle and highly effective and are generally accepted common attitudes: no one questions their desirability; no one challenges the implicit discrimination.

These are the perceptions that place women at a disadvantage in competition with men in the marketplace: the perception of inferior capacity; the perception of lack of initiative; the perception that women are by nature limited to low-level activities directed by men; the perception that it is unnatural to expect to find women in high-level positions in business, government, and the professions. A United States Presidential Task Force on Women's Rights and Responsibilities concluded that discriminatory practices against women have been so widespread and pervasive that they have come to be regarded as normal.[1]

The presence of some women in high-level activities is commonly viewed as an aberration, a chance occurrence, a politically motivated token, nepotism, a favour. The almost complete dominance of desirable employment positions by men has created the perception among women of a tacit understanding among men to exclude them from positions of authority. The employment structure is perceived in oligopolistic terms with barriers to entry into the high levels of the hierarchical structure, collusive arrangements among men on hiring and promotions, and tacit understanding to exclude women from the decision-making processes whenever they become a potential threat to continued male dominance.

An examination of men's and women's employment will establish that the two sexes tend to be engaged in different activities: most men are employed in occupations in which men predominate; most women are employed in occupations in which women predominate. There are virtually no occupations and employments in which men and women are equally represented. They work together, yet they are divided.

Further examination will establish that the occupations in which women predominate are not as well paid as those in which men predominate. Few women will be found in the very high-paid employments; very few will be found in the high-skill blue-collar occupations of mechanic, machinist, electronics technician; and notwithstanding the very substantial increase of women in professional occupations and management positions in the past two decades, very few of them will be found at the higher levels of their occupations.[2]

What accounts for the different distribution of men and women within the employment structure? Does it reflect free choices motivated by different career expectations or discriminatory practices in admissions to educational and training programs and in hiring and promotions? The prevailing view, even among women, appears to be that the distribution reflects free choice within the range of occupations preferred by women. This raises some very critical questions. Why should women "prefer" low-paid office work over the more highly paid occupations of mechanic, technician, electrician, plumber, carpenter, truck driver, and other occupations in which men predominate? Is it the additional education and training that such occupations require? Is it the nature of the work activities in which they engage? Is it the respective work environments and range of associations at work? Is it the hours of work and the greater flexibility in working hours and time-off periods? Is it the expectation of lesser conflict with household and family responsibilities? Is it the expectation that it is easier to enter and exit, re-enter and re-exit such employments? Do women have different values than men in relation to success and money? All of these have been found to affect decisions on occupational and employment choices.[3] But what may appear as "preferences" may not in fact be the preferred employments, and what may appear as "free choices" may not in fact be choices freely made. The range of occupations to which women have access may be limited, which would limit the range of preferences and choices. These preferences and choices may be dictated by social criteria of "appropriate" vocations for women, and they may be dictated, as well, by generally accepted limitations in the capacities of women to undertake and perform certain work functions.

It is not easy to distinguish between reality and fiction in long-established and generally accepted perceptions and practices in the occupational allocation of men and women and in the assignment to them of work responsibilities. Which of the observed differences between men and women in actual and potential performance of work functions at various levels are physiologically based, and which are the result of social conditioning? For example, can women be as effective fighter pilots, fire fighters, and police officers as men have been? This is a subject for continuing investigation and experiment. Ultimately, demonstrations will establish what is fiction, formulated and propagated by men to reduce potential competition, and what is reality.

As long as women are perceived to have different capabilities than men, and the perceived differences are not challenged with demonstrated evidence, women will remain typecast and disadvantaged in the market. Typecasting provides rationale for segregation and differential values to the work in which women engage. The characterization of women as good or not so good for this or that activity suggests implicitly the nature of activities in which men expect women to engage, and by implication the nature of activities in which they expect to find women at work. Such attitudes influence the nature of work assigned to women and the values placed on such work. Even where women have negated preconceived notions about their abilities and potentialities and have entered occupations long associated with men, lingering notions of perceived weaknesses result in the assignment to them of lower-level work responsibilities and the payment of correspondingly lower salaries.

That women are discriminated against in employment is incontestable: discrimination occurs in the selection, interviewing, and hiring process, in the assignment of work responsibilities, in promotions, and in pay. Denial of this reality will not contribute to our understanding of the fundamental elements responsible for its existence or to developing corrective initiatives, which are needed if we are to reduce and ultimately eliminate the inequities and inefficiencies inherent in discrimination.

The question is "what corrective initiatives?" The answer will be found in the variables that make discrimination possible – the market conditions that make it possible for employers to discriminate and cause employees to accept discriminatory employment practices. Such discrimination is not possible in competitive markets at full employment, which suggests that discriminatory practices have their roots in market imperfections – market conditions that enable employers to discriminate among potential employees in hiring and among their employees in promotion and pay; and supply conditions, such as excessive unemployment, that disadvantage potential employees in the marketplace and cause them to accept terms and conditions of employment they know to be discriminatory. In this context, the corrective initiatives must identify the imperfections on both the demand (employer) side and supply (employee) side of the market and make an effort to remove them. It is critical to recognize that there are two sides to the discriminatory process, and for discrimination to take place one or the other side must have an advantage: employers cannot discriminate if employees are in a position to refuse terms and conditions of employment known to them to be discriminatory.

But one imperfection seems to override market conditions: *the ethic of discrimination.* This is manifested in employment and pay practices that are known to be discriminatory yet are accepted as normal in the context of prevailing economic and social behaviour. When a practice becomes widespread and is accepted as normal, it is often deemed to be socially sanctioned. Socially sanctioned practices are difficult to eradicate. Legislative measures can identify them and declare them unlawful but cannot end them. Legislation cannot create an ethic of equal opportunity; it can only provide for the observance of socially acceptable standards. When the socially acceptable standards are discriminatory, the role of prohibitive legislation is a declaration of an alternative political standard. The effectiveness of such legislation is conditional on the convergence of the social standard and the political standard. Society must recognize that *the ethic of discrimination* violates fundamental values of fairness and equity.

The ethic of equal opportunity should be accepted as gender neutral: employment qualifications, initiative, productivity, and the potential of individual persons, not the person's sex, should determine opportunity.

Although legislation cannot create an ethic of equal opportunity, it can remove barriers to equal opportunity. Legislation can redress unequal opportunities to educational and training programs, to desirable employment positions, and to upward mobility within employment; legislation can also effect change in the problem of unequal pay for work of equal value. Government pronouncements and exhortations alone will not bring an end to segregation and discrimination in employment, promotion, and wages. In a society where self-interest governs transactive relationships, voluntarism is not the road to equity and economic justice. Governments must become interventionist on behalf of the disadvantaged. It is not adequate to declare that equality is incorporated in the Charter of Rights and Freedoms and leave the onus with the aggrieved to seek redress with human rights commissions and the legal system. In a market economy, governed largely by free interactive and transactive relationships, only the very independent of mind and of resources dare challenge the established authority of enterprises and employers. Human rights commissions are remote, and the legal system is cumbersome, complex, and costly.

Furthermore, commissions and courts are not competent on matters of employment, equal opportunity, pay equity, and the economic and social conditions that enter into the decisions subject to challenge. The barriers women face will not be overcome through a legal and quasi-legal system that requires the scaling of even higher barriers for access to it. An alternative system, which will not only administer the relevant legislation but also evolve a code of ethical behaviour in employment, must be established. Such a system must be community-based, must be constituted of employer, employee, and community representatives, and must be freely accessible to all men and women who feel aggrieved in their employment relationships.

The chapters that follow examine many of the issues that concern women in paid employment: the explanations commonly given for discriminatory practices; the myths about women that provide the bases for different perceptions of them in the marketplace than the perceptions of men in the marketplace; the occupational distribution of women and the possible reasons for a distribution that differs significantly from that of men; the changes in occupational distribution that have taken place and are likely to take place as a result of the advent of computer technology; the threats to the employment of women in an increasingly competitive labour market; and the ways in which women have responded both to discriminatory employment practices and to the challenges of the emerging age of computer technology.

Notes

1. Juanita Kreps, *Sex in the Marketplace: American Women at Work* (Baltimore: Johns Hopkins Press, 1971), p. 92.
2. J-A Boulet and L. Lavalee, *The Changing Economic Status of Women*, Economic Council of Canada (Ottawa: Supply and Services Canada, 1984); Daniel Boothby, *Women Reentering*

the Labour Force and Training Programmes: Evidence from Canada, Economic Council of Canada (Ottawa: Supply and Services Canada, 1986).
3. A good summary of these and other explanations will be found in Sharon Shepela and Ann Viviano, "Some Psychological Factors Affecting Job Segregation and Wages," in Helen Remick, ed., *Comparable Worth and Wage Discrimination* (Philadelphia: Temple University Press, 1984), pp. 47-58; Paula England, "Socioeconomic Explanations of Job Segregation," *ibid.*, pp. 28-46; A. Bella, "Occupational Segregations by Sex: Determinants and Changes," *Journal of Human Resources*, 17, 3 (1982), 371-92.

1

Accounting for Discrimination

The Dual Role Issue

Any examination of the role and experience of women in the labour market would be inadequate if it did not approach the subject from the standpoint of the dual responsibility of employed women – the responsibilities assigned to them in their paid employment and those associated with the position of wife and mother. "Women's paid employment does not exist in isolation," wrote a group of British researchers; "it is inextricably linked to women's unpaid work in the household and the community."[1] The fact is that women the world over have primary responsibility for the non-material well-being of their families. Therefore, the decisions of women to enter educational and training programs designed to prepare them for paid employment and to enter the labour market and seek paid employment entail trade-offs that involve implicit and explicit costs. This is particularly the case with married women and women with children. Whether the assignment of primary responsibility to women for family and home is right or wrong, desirable or undesirable, fair or unfair, just or unjust, is not the issue: it is a fact in almost all countries, regardless of their political and economic systems. As long as this remains a fact of family life, women who decide to or who feel they must enter into paid employment face the dilemma of balancing the responsibilities of paid work with those they implicitly assume upon marriage and having children. A fundamental principle in contract theory is that the parties entering into a voluntary contractual relationship expect to be better off with it than without it. To the extent that some women end up worse off in their marriage contracts, it can be assumed that they entered into marriage blind to the reality of the actual relationship or that conditions so changed in the interim as to turn positive expectations into negative outcomes. The solution to such a problem is, of course, the termination of the contractual relationship, but that is not easy when the relationship has evolved into one of material dependence and the existence of children.

In the past, tradition had it that a wife's and mother's place was in the home; women who wished to make work outside the home a career, as in teaching and nursing, for example, were to remain single. In the early 1950s, the director of nursing of a city hospital called to her office one of her young nurses, who had indicated that she contemplated marriage, and said to her, "But you can't get married, Miss E, we need nurses!" Marriage was deemed incompatible with full-time work, particularly with work that involved long hours, over the twenty-four-hour cycle, any six days of the week. Furthermore, work after marriage was interpreted within some ethnic groups to mean that the young husband could not support his wife, a stigma that often led to social ostracism.

Attitudes have changed over the past few decades. More education and more widespread education contributed to the change, and so has the change in working conditions. Hours of work per day and per week have become fewer, and so have the days of work per week. With good organization of work in the household economy and allocation of work within the household in accordance with the principles of the division of labour, it should be possible to participate actively and effectively in both the household economy and the market economy. The increasing capitalization of household production will make this even more possible than it is at present. Therefore, increasing participation by women in the market economy, full-time and continuous over work-life, is the trend of the future.

There is a presumption in all this, of course, that people must necessarily be involved in both the household economy and the market economy. That is a contestable presumption. It is possible to transfer most activities of the household economy to the market economy; and it is equally possible to expand the household economy. The notion that work in the household economy is degrading and humiliating to the individual and wasteful to society and the economy, while work in the market economy is stimulating to the individual and socially productive, is a gross distortion of reality. Most of the work performed in the market economy is neither stimulating nor satisfying; most of it is supervised drudgery. The difference is not in the nature and value of the work; it is rather in the respective work environments and in the payment for the work. If the organization of household work were to provide for social interaction similar to that provided in the market economy and if a system of valuation and payment for household work were to be established, many of the work activities in the household economy would gain a competitive advantage over work performed in the market economy.

Entry/Exit and Competition

In the theory of factor substitution – the substitution of people with machines, of men with women – the determinant of the rate of substitution is the product-price ratios of the competing factors over time. That is, the productivity-price ratio of the capital equipment relative to the productivity-price (wage) ratio of the workers to be displaced; the productivity-price (wage) ratio of one worker (man) relative to the productivity-price (wage) ratio of another worker (woman). The factor that will be used will be that which has the higher ratio.

Entry/exit rates and the length of stay out of the workplace are the most critical variables in the determination of competitiveness and substitutability between men and women. In the calculation of *potential* productivity, account is taken of the continuity of service with the organization, the broadness of experience at different levels of activity, demonstrated initiative, reliability, demonstrated capacity to work with others constructively and beneficially, and so on. In many of these areas, men exceed women much of the time, particularly in relation to continuity of service and broadness of experience, both of which are affected negatively by interruptions in employment.

Entry/exit rates for women have decreased over time but continue to be relatively high, and periods of separation have been relatively long and are expected to lengthen with the introduction of maternity leaves with job and pay guarantees. A 1975 U.S. study[2] determined that only about *one-third* of employed white women between ages 18 and 64 had worked continuously since the completion of their schooling. The proportion of the 30-45 age group was only *one-quarter*.

The study found also that periods of entry/exit and re-entry varied significantly: 20 per cent delayed their entry into the labour market an average of 9.6 years after completion of their schooling; 15 per cent entered employment upon completion of schooling, worked for a while, and then withdrew and stayed out for an average of 8.2 years. On re-entry into the market they remained in employment thereafter continuously. Finally, 20 per cent entered, exited, re-entered, and re-exited two or more times, and each time they stayed out varying periods. The remainder did not enter the market at all or entered for varying periods upon completion of schooling, exited, and remained out of the market.

Continuity in work activity, in work associations, and in work relationships with others – within the organization and in other organizations, with buyers and sellers, clients and suppliers – is regarded very highly in the assessment of employees. Separations, discontinuities, and disassociations from work affect productivity and generally are regarded negatively in organizations. Therefore, attention should be focused on ways to reduce the length of separation where desirable and possible, and to somehow reduce the discontinuity and disassociation that separation has entailed. If it were possible to continue some involvement with the work process and some partial association with the organization during separation, the effects on efficiency may not be as negative. Computers and telecommunications technologies provide such a possibility.

Conditions Predisposing Discrimination

A number of conditions predispose discriminatory practices against women: one is the predominance of women in *ancillary work activities*, commonly under the direction of men; even in some professions where women predominate, such as nursing, they are regarded as the assistants (helpers) of men, and not as independent workers.

The second condition predisposing discrimination is the notion that women are *supplementary family workers*, whose earnings are intended to supplement the family income, which is implicitly presumed to be adequate. This is reflected in the not infrequent practices of laying off married women first when staff reductions are introduced and of hiring unemployed men who support families.

A third condition is the notion that *the productivity of women* is generally lower than that of men, a notion that finds support in the alleged lower motivation of women in work outside the home and in the conflicting responsibilities of home, family, and work. It is not humanly possible, it is said, to be a mother, a homemaker, and a full-time worker and remain efficient in all three. Something has to suffer, and it is usually the work activity outside the family and home that suffers. This is not the case with all women, of course. But the association of women with primary responsibility for family and home provides substance to the argument.

Some women have chosen to make their market employment their career employment and have taken the necessary steps to accommodate the claims on their time and effort by home and family so that neither career nor home and family would be impaired. Many such women have been successful in their careers. The majority of women, however, elect or feel compelled to combine full-time market employment and full-time home employment, which results from time to time, if not all the time, in inadequate performance in one, the other, or both. Persistent, even though periodic, inadequate performance impairs progress in the world of work.

A fourth condition accounting for the relatively slow progress of women in the marketplace is the *frequent discontinuity* of many women in active participation and the consequent failure to gain the seniority and experience gained by those who remain in employment continuously without prolonged interruptions. In the highly competitive world of internal labour markets[3] in individual enterprises, continuous presence within the daily work environment is critical to vertical mobility. Departures from the environment of daily decision-making, even for such routine absences as vacations, place people at a competitive disadvantage relative to those who are present when emerging problems are discussed and decisions are taken.

Reasons for Occupational Segregation

Historically, much of the occupational segregation of men and women has been attributed to two realities: the *functional* reality in the workplace, which involved long hours, heavy work, taxing work environments; and the *role differentiation* between men and women, which imposed on men the responsibility to labour in mines, on the land, in manufacturing processes, in transportation and construction in order to provide the means of subsistence for their families, while women specialized in work at home, including the bearing and rearing of children.[4]

The two realities have changed significantly over the past few decades. *In relation to the functional reality*, a relatively small proportion of the labour force is now engaged in work involving long hours of heavy work in mines, construction, transportation, and manufacturing processes. Most of the traditionally male jobs can now be accomplished by women, too, with equal and in some instances perhaps greater efficiency and effectiveness. In other words, the functional reality of work and places of work has changed so much over the decades as to increase the potential range of substitutability between men and women in many work activities. The barrier is no longer related to the functional aspects of the work; it will be found rather in custom, in legal and institutional regulations and practices, and in the threat that women of superior intellect present to men of average ability occupying responsible positions.

The increasing participation by women in occupations from which they were virtually excluded in the past, such as accounting, law, medicine, engineering, business management, and the traditional trades, is the first phase in the process of desegregation. But recognition and acceptance of substitutability between men and women will not occur until women are given the opportunity to demonstrate the range of their abilities in their chosen occupations.

The functional activities associated with individual occupations are wide-ranging. Therefore, access into an occupation does not in itself mean perfect substitutability over the entire range of activities. It is possible to provide access, but to limit the range of substitution to the lowest functions. This is the experience of many women who have entered heretofore male-dominated occupations, particularly in the professions. They have been admitted, but limited to the lowest levels of the professional work functions.

The second phase in the process of desegregation must break the barriers to the higher ranges of functional activities within individual occupations. Access to the entire range of work and responsibility is critical to the attainment of complete substitutability within occupations and administrative (managerial) structures. The paucity of women in the high echelons in government, in private and public institutions, in the professions, and in commerce can be explained in large part on the basis of functional barriers. Barriers to entry have been lowered in many male-dominated occupations, but functional barriers have continued to limit women to the lower levels within these occupations.

Role differentiation, which limited women in our society to activities related to home and family, has largely passed into history. It is no longer socially degrading to husbands and wives, fathers and daughters, for women to work for pay in the marketplace.

The notion that work should be allocated on the basis of sex, that some work activities are suitable for men and some suitable for women, is imbedded in the cultures and practices of all societies. In some societies women do the heavy work, such as gathering and transporting wood and tilling and cultivating the land; in other societies women are limited to household activities.

Custom-based occupational choices within a society give the impression of being free choices. Girls "choose" nursing and teaching, whereas boys choose medicine and engineering. When some girls choose medicine and engineering, it is viewed as an exception, an aberration to generally accepted practice. The choices appear to be free; yet they are often dictated by underlying social forces of greater strength and authority than any legislative dictum. Custom has no compassion, does not recognize ability and proficiency, and does not respond easily to change; those responsible for the perpetuation of customary practices in employment usually reap high economic rents.

The underlying hidden forces that dictate discriminatory choices are found on both the supply side of the market and on the demand side: on the supply side, girls are expected to enter occupations generally recognized as appropriate for women; on the demand side, employers are expected to assign responsibilities deemed appropriate for women. The general social acceptance of discriminatory choices over time tends to legitimize discrimination. When that happens, the discriminated groups evolve employment characteristics appropriate to their own conditions and preferences, which become very effective entry barriers. Women are reluctant to seek entry into male-dominated environments; men are reluctant to enter employments dominated by women.

Employment and Discrimination

In the past two decades, women have entered male-dominated occupations in increasing numbers. Although they continue to crowd in traditionally female jobs, such as clerical and general services, increasing numbers are found in medicine, law, accounting, engineering, and general management. Between 1971 and 1981, employment of women in clerical and general low-paid service jobs increased by about 60 per cent, while their employment in managerial positions increased by 247 per cent, and the number of women lawyers increased by 556 per cent, physicians and surgeons, 140 per cent, engineers, 534 per cent, accountants, almost 180 per cent. (Detailed information on this will be found in Table 7.1.)

Notwithstanding these numbers, however, evidence of continuing segregation is overwhelming: as with racial, ethnic, and other minority groups, women are expected to have academic qualifications and experience superior to those of the men with whom they compete, and they are expected to accept lower pay than that of men with inferior qualifications. The onus is on women to prove themselves, and the "proof" is not that which an average man can do well, but that which a superior man can do well. Still, by showing such capacity, the best a woman can expect is to be assigned responsibilities appropriate to the average male worker.

In considering discriminatory behaviour, we must distinguish between occupational discrimination and discrimination in employment. *Occupational discrimination* relates to access into educational and training programs; *employment discrimination* refers to access to employment opportunities and to the assignment of responsibilities upon the securing of employment. It is quite possible for a woman to experience no occupational discrimination but then to face serious employment discrimination upon the acquisition of occupational qualifications. Indeed, such has been the case in recent years with certain professional occupations: academic institutions have provided equal access to men and women in certain of their programs, such as commerce, law, and medicine, yet their women graduates have encountered difficulties finding suitable employment with their precertification training. Upon certification, however, they have encountered difficulties in finding employment appropriate to their qualifications, and, upon finding employment, they have faced difficulties in gaining responsibilities commensurate with their qualifications and experience.

It appears that competitive access into high-level educational programs and the successful completion of such programs have not been matched by access to appropriate employment positions and progression within the employment structure. Barriers to employment appropriate to educational qualification are widespread, and there are additional barriers to progress and promotion within the employment structure. This suggests that the focus must now shift from educational barriers, which have been hurdled, to the barriers that make entry into and progression within appropriate employments difficult for women. Organizations and enterprises must recognize the very substantial costs they bear in not utilizing optimally the talents and capacities of their female employees.

What Motivates Discrimination?

Occupational and employment discrimination is founded on three motivations: *prejudice, tradition,* and *economic advantage.*[5] Discrimination based on prejudice is of a personal nature. The employer simply does not wish to employ women, or men do not wish to work with women, or customers do not wish to be attended by women. They hold negative judgements about women, which cannot be supported by competent evidence but which are valid in their own minds. Discrimination based on tradition, on the other hand, may not have the personal element; it may well be imposed on the employer, who may be inclined to act otherwise in its absence.

The most despicable form of discrimination is that practised for economic advantage: the employer is aware of the discriminatory behaviour, knows that it cannot be justified on economic grounds, but abides by the prevailing practice for economic gain. The payment of different wages to men and women for the same work, the assignment of work responsibilities to women that exceed the specifications of their jobs and their range of pay, and the failure to give women employment designations commensurate with their functional activities in order to justify their lower pay are but a few of the forms of discrimination for economic gain.

Discrimination in the assignment of work responsibilities and discrimination in the make-up of policy-making committees are the most insidious forms of discrimination. Women are denied the experience needed for senior managerial and administrative positions, and they are denied the breadth of experience that often provides economic justification for differences in pay.[6] To the extent that pay is based on relative contributions to output and different employment positions make different contributions, discrimination in the assignment of employment responsibilities provides economic justification for discrimination in pay. In other words, if one were to assume that the respective tasks of men and women were appropriate and that their pay reflected the contribution of each to the process, then the respective tasks would be adjudged to be efficient and equitable. The inefficiency and inequity would be hidden in the initial decision on employment assignments.

Consider the following example: a bank hires two commerce graduates with equal academic qualifications. The male graduate is assigned to the loans department, while the female is placed in the traditional tellers' department. The difference in pay between the two positions may well be justified on the basis of the estimated respective contributions of the two to the value of the banking process. The inequity is not in the pay but in the assigned employment responsibilities. From the standpoint of the initial allocation of the two to the employment activities, both efficiency and equity are violated in the sense that *the potential* of the female graduate is being underutilized. Economic theory postulates that in a competitive market women will move out of the employments in which they are underutilized and seek out jobs which will utilize their capacities. But such equilibrium will not be achieved in a market that is not very competitive and in which segregation is a widespread employment practice.

This form of segregation, which underutilizes the capacities of women, is also widespread within occupations. Although women have been admitted in heretofore male-dominated occupations in increasing numbers, they have been held largely at the lower levels of the occupational ladders: few of them are found in the upper echelons in medicine, law, accounting, engineering, or management. Even in the public sector, which is presumed to be less discriminatory, the number of women in high administrative positions is relatively small. Similarly, although increasing numbers have been admitted into management, for the most part they have been limited to the middle management levels.

Work Assignments and Pay

From an economic standpoint, the most negative form of discrimination is the assignment to women of work activities that underutilize their productive capacities. The emphasis on pay discrimination is misplaced. Whether men and women are paid the same for work of equal value is of lesser importance than whether men and women with the same qualifications are viewed as equal in the assignment of work responsibilities. Upon examination it will be found that the *implicit* pay discrimination as a result of discrimination in the assignment of work responsibilities is significantly greater than the actual pay discrimination related to work of equal value. It is the appointment of the man to the position of loans officer and the woman to the position of teller, or the expectation of higher qualifications from women than from men for the same work assignments, that are critical to the issues of efficiency and equity, not the payment of different wages for work of equal value. On the basis of equity and efficiency, it is easier to justify differences in pay for work of equal value, defined in terms of skill, effort, responsibility, and conditions of work, than it is to justify differences in pay as a result of discrimination in the assignment of work responsibilities. The one may be justified on the basis of differences in productivity; the other may reflect a loss in potential output.

Federal legislation[7] on the matter is aimed at differences in pay for work of equal value. It prohibits employers from having different wages for male and female employees in the same establishment who are performing work of equal value. It requires employers to assess "the value of work" performed in different employment activities within individual establishments on the basis of the composite of skill, effort, and responsibility required in the performance of the work and the conditions under which the work is performed, and to ensure that the differences in wages reflect the differences in the value of work. The underlying assumption is that with the establishment of criteria for the determination of "work of equal value" and the requirement that work assignments of equal value should be paid equal wages, the monetary rationale for occupational segregation will be eliminated. The question then would be whether employers will continue to discriminate between men and women in the assignment of work responsibilities if there were no monetary advantage to discriminate. If they continued to discriminate on the basis of perceived differences between men and women in the execution of work assignments, then segregation will continue and employers will bear the cost of it, which would be the difference between the wages they believe should exist and the absence of any wage difference.

The objective, of course, should not be to penalize the employer for discriminating in pay, since pay discrimination may be justified on the basis of differences in productivity. The same composites of skill, effort, and responsibility at different levels of the occupational structure and at different stages of the production process do not necessarily result in the same value added.[8] Therefore, the objective should be to cause employers not to discriminate in the assignment of work responsibilities. Evidence will show that women place greater significance to this aspect of the employment process than to differences in pay. Although critical references to differences in pay are frequent, differences in work assignments that reflect discriminatory decisions are subject to more widespread comment. There is a greater sense of unfairness in discriminatory assignments of work responsibilities than there is in pay discrimination.

Pay discrimination and discrimination in work assignments are linked in a causal relationship: discrimination in the assignment of work responsibilities tends to crowd women in work activities deemed appropriate for them, which results in excess supply of women in such activities. The excess supply relative to demand tends to keep their pay depressed. Thus, discrimination in work assignments provides market justification for the differences in pay.

The distinction between pay discrimination and discrimination in work assignments has yet another significance: pay discrimination may be market determined and therefore may be claimed to be imposed by impersonal market forces, yet discrimination in work assignments is the result of deliberate human decisions. When women crowd at certain levels of professional, managerial, and other work activities and few of them advance to the higher levels, it is because they are not assigned the responsibilities that would give them the depth and breadth of work experience deemed necessary for wider and higher levels of work responsibility.

As we search for ways to end pay discrimination, it is well to distinguish between pay differences for the same kind of work and pay discrimination. *Pay differences* for the same kind of work would not be discriminatory if they reflect differences in productivity. *Pay discrimination* means different wages and salaries are paid to men and women doing the same kind of work and making the same contributions to output, or that the differences in wages and salaries do not reflect the differences in productivity.

Efficiency dictates that payment reflect relative productivities. If the differences in wages and salaries do not reflect the differences in productivity, resources will be misallocated and economic efficiency will be impaired.[9] The implication of this for efforts to reduce differences in pay between men and women doing the same kind of work is to determine whether the pay differences reflect differences in productivity. If they do, then efforts must be directed toward the equalization of productivity. In other words, efforts at equality in pay should focus on equal opportunities for men and women to participate in the broad range of work activities now more readily available to men than to women. Equal opportunities over the entire range of activities for which they qualify will reduce the underutilization of the capacities of women, which will bring about equalization in pay.

Internal Labour Markets

The link between wages and discrimination in work assignments and the crowding of women in some occupations at low levels of employment provide an economic interpretation to the arguments of the so-called institutionalists in labour market analysis.[10] The common interpretation of the arguments of institutionalists is that they have challenged the primacy of demand and supply in determination of wages and attributed wage determination instead to the internal policies and practices of individual enterprises. Large enterprises in particular are deemed to function within their organizational systems as replicas of the external labour market, with all the characteristics of external labour markets – their internal wage and salary structures, their systems of training and retraining, selection of employees for various activities, competition among employees, internal mobility, promotions and demotions. It is alleged that the criteria used by enterprises in the management of their workers are dominated by institutional practices, custom, and other "non-economic" variables. Yet, on examination it will be found that the non-economic variables often provide economic justifications for the outcomes. If the custom of the enterprise dictates that women be assigned work activities "appropriate" for women and that results in crowding of women in certain work activities, the crowding provides the economic rationale for the low wages they receive.

The implication of this for the end of wage discrimination is clear: end discrimination in the assignment of work responsibilities within enterprises. It is particularly important that such discrimination be prevented at the time of initial entry into employment, as well as at each progressive phase of the employment experience. This is a difficult task, but perhaps less difficult than the development of criteria on the "work of equal value" concept. It is less difficult to develop mechanisms and procedures for the objective evaluation of the qualifications and experience of men and women for the assignment of work responsibilities than to develop criteria that will approximate the relative values of work among diverse forms of economic activity.

Forms of Discrimination

Economists have examined extensively the various forms of discriminatory practices. Gary Becker examined the issue from the standpoint of prejudice by employers, employees, and customers toward some group in the labour force and the effect of that on the wage: employers who are prejudiced against women will hire them only if there is an incentive to do so, such as a lower wage than they would pay to men; employees who are prejudiced against women and dislike working with them will do so if they are given an incentive, such as a wage premium; and customers who are prejudiced against women and dislike being served by them will deal with women if they are given an incentive, such as a lower price, which becomes reflected in the lower pay for women.[11] The wage differential between men and women that arises from such discriminating behaviour is designated by Becker as *discrimination coefficient 'd'*. The size of the discrimination coefficient 'd' manifests the degree of discriminatory behaviour and the offsetting wage incentive: male workers may demand a very substantial wage premium to work with women in traditional "male jobs," yet may not expect any differential if they are working with women in jobs that are known as "women's jobs," notwithstanding the cost of pride in the latter instance.

Discriminatory behaviour and the consequent wage differences that manifest it lead to two possible outcomes that warrant a brief comment. First, the employer may not profit from the discriminatory behaviour: the prejudiced workers who demand offsetting premiums and the prejudiced customers who demand offsetting reduced prices may be the ones who profit. The other possible outcome is that the employer who feels he must pay discriminatory premiums may gain by employing more women.

Barbara Bergmann developed the thesis of *occupational crowding*, whereby discriminated groups crowd into certain occupations and become cross-identified with those occupations.[12] Crowding results, of course, in excess supply relative to demand in the indicated occupations, which keeps their wages depressed relative to occupations that are not so designated. The same thesis applies to the consequences of the *market segmentation* hypothesis developed by Michael Piore and Peter Doeringer.[13] They identify two distinct labour markets: a *primary market*, which is structured, organized into protective unions and associations, monopolistic, governed by the internal rules of associations and enterprises, and a *secondary market*, which is unorganized, crowded, highly competitive, unstable, subordinated. For the most part, the primary market is predominantly male, the secondary predominantly female.

Edmund Phelps is associated with the *statistical discrimination* hypothesis, which postulates that discrimination emanates from testing procedures designed to determine potential productivity.[14] But, intentionally or unintentionally, the testing procedures are biased against some groups – sex-biased, language-biased, culture-biased. Finally, Lester Thurow is associated with the proposition of *implicit pay discrimination*, which postulates that pay differences result from discrimination in access to social human capital – access to education and training.[15] Although this is more of an explanation for inequalities in income distribution than of pay discrimination between men and women, to the extent that women have been barred in the past from entry into some educational and training programs, and to the extent that women are not given equal opportunities to develop their talents, the resultant pay differences may be deemed to represent implicit pay discrimination.

The evidence indicates that discrimination takes a number of forms: there is *occupational discrimination*, whereby entry into the educational and training programs leading to certain occupational qualifications is limited; there is, as well, *employment discrimination*, whereby women are not welcomed into certain work activities, even though they may have the requisite occupational qualifications. The combined effect of occupational discrimination and employment discrimination is the segregation of women in a few occupations, which results in *crowding*, with negative effects on their wages and other terms and conditions of employment. To these we add the practice of widespread *discrimination in the assignment of work functions* within enterprises (within internal labour markets), which determine the nature and range of work experience women receive. Since the nature and range of work experience is the most critical criterion for promotions to high-level positions, discrimination in the assignment of work explains the virtual absence of women from senior positions in commercial, industrial, and institutional enterprises, including governments and governmental institutions. The extent of this absence is examined in the next chapter.

Discrimination takes many other forms: the tendency to require higher educational and experience qualifications from discriminated groups; the use of biased instruments and procedures in the determination of potential for employment, for promotion, for the assignment of work responsibilities;[16] and, of course, outright discrimination based on age, marital status, physical appearance, colour of skin, and so on.

Response of Women to Discrimination in Employment

Women have responded to discrimination in a traditional manner, that is, they have entered those areas of work left open to them and those for which they have specific aptitudes and endowments; they have acquired more education and training than required of the non-discriminated groups; and they have gone into independent employment as professionals and proprietors. The last two are particularly important, since they have been used as countervailing measures, attempts to use education and entrepreneurship to offset discriminatory practices – sort of a positive discrimination coefficient intended to override the negative discrimination coefficient associated with gender and the implicit difference in degrees of responsibility, effectiveness, and efficiency. When equals in education are perceived to be unequal in performance, then one way to equalize the performance is to make education unequal in an offseting way. This appears to have worked to some degree: women have achieved positions that were closed to them; with MBA degrees they have got to levels of the occupational hierarchy held with BA degrees. A detailed examination of the response by women to discrimination and to threats on their employment will be found in Chapter 7.

Notes

1. Charlotte Huggett *et al.*, "Microelectronics and the Jobs Women Do," in W. Faulkner and E. Arnold, *Smothered by Invention – Technology in Women's Lives* (London: Pluto Press, 1985), p. 200.
2. Mary Corcoran, "The Structure of Female Wages," *American Economic Review: Papers and Proceedings* (May, 1978), pp. 165-70. See also Jacob Mincer and Haim Ofek, "Interrupted Work Careers: Depreciation and Restoration of Human Capital, " *Journal of Human Resources*, XVII (Winter, 1982). They found interruptions in work activity with prolonged periods of non-participation have negative effects on skills and efficiency. But the level of efficiency is restored within relatively short periods.
3. P. Doeringer and M. Piore, *Internal Labor Markets and Manpower Analysis* (Lexington, Mass.: D. C. Heath, 1971).
4. Victor R. Fuchs, "Recent Trends and Long-run Prospects for Female Earnings," *American Economic Review*, 64, 2 (May, 1974), pp. 236-42.
5. These three forms of prejudice are identified by Gary Becker in *The Economics of Discrimination* (Chicago: University of Chicago Press, 1971).
6. Robin L. Bartlett and Timothy I. Miller, "Executive Compensation: Female Executives and Networking," *American Economic Review: Papers and Proceedings*, 75, 2 (May, 1985), pp. 266-70.
7. Human Rights Act, Section II (2).
8. Roberta E. Robb, "Conceptual and Operational Issues Confronting the Equal Value Approach to Equal Pay," a presentation to the Colloquium on the Economic Status of Women in the Labour Market, Economic Council of Canada, Montreal, Nov. 26-28, 1984, pp. 5-6.
9. Paul Miller has carried out some tests on this matter. See "Gender Differences in Observed and Offered Wages in Canada, 1980," *Canadian Journal of Economics* (May, 1987), pp. 225-44.
10. Doeringer and Piore, *Internal Labor Markets*; R. Edwards, M. Reich, and D. Gordon, eds., *Labour Market Segmentations* (Lexington, Mass.: D.C. Heath, 1975).
11. Becker, *The Economics of Discrimination.*
12. Barbara Bergmann, "The Effect on White Incomes of Discrimination in Employment," *Journal of Political Economy*, 79, 2 (March/April, 1971), pp. 294-313.
13. Doeringer and Piore, *Internal Labour Markets.*
14. Edmund Phelps, "The Theory of Racism and Sexism," *American*

Economic Review (September, 1972), pp. 659-61.

15. Lester C. Thurow, *Generating Inequality: Mechanisms of Distribution in the U.S. Economy* (New York: Basic Books, 1975).

16. The issue of sex-biased, culture-biased, and language-biased instruments and procedures is discussed by Phelps in "The Theory of Racism and Sexism."

2

Myths about Women

Introduction

Four myths about women are largely responsible for their secondary role in the labour market and for the persistence of low wages and salaries relative to those of men.[1] *The first myth* is that most women enter into paid employment to supplement the family income and buy some "extras" for themselves and their families – "pin money." In reality, most women have worked, in paid employment, in family enterprises, on farms and vegetable gardens, and, of course, in unpaid activities related to family and home. The notion that women work for "pin money" has no basis in fact. In addition to those who need to supplement the family income, there are those who need to earn their own income and those who must earn the family income. In 1986, some 676,000 women in the labour force were heads of family units and 759,000 were unattached persons, which means they were not members of family units. Also, 392,000 had husbands who were either unemployed or were not in the labour force. These total 1,827,000, which is about one-third of the number of women in the labour force in 1986.

The second myth is that women are not committed to employment in the marketplace, that their commitment is to family and home. Yet, of the 4,977,000 women in paid employment in 1986, almost 29 per cent (1,466,000) had worked at their jobs 1-5 years, about 20 per cent (978,000) had their jobs 6-10 years, 16 per cent (790,000) were at their jobs 11-20 years, and 5 per cent (237,000) had their jobs over 20 years.[2] Such facts hardly convey the impression of occasional, temporary employment with no long-term commitment to work. By contrast, of the 6,657,000 men in employment in 1986 about 25 per cent (1,640,000) held their jobs 1-5 years, 18 per cent 6-10 years, 20 per cent 11-20 years, and 13 per cent over 20 years – somewhat higher proportions in long-term employment, but not as high in relation to those of women as one would expect from the general impression of women having primarily short-term, casual, and occasional employment. The statistical information indicates that such impressions are not founded on reality. Whether the decision to enter and remain in paid employment is motivated by financial or non-financial considerations is of little consequence: the important fact is that increasing numbers of women – single, married, divorced, separated, with husbands present and not present, with very young children and older children – enter into paid employment at various ages and remain in paid employment without interruptions over long periods of time.

A *third myth* is that women prefer part-time employment. While it is true that a significantly larger proportion of women than men hold part-time jobs (7.8 per cent of employed men, 26 per cent of employed women in 1986), that is often a matter of compelled circumstance for many women, not a matter of preference. As long as women remain largely responsible for the work involved in the maintenance of family and home, they will be limited in the amount of work they can do outside the home. Depending on the nature and size of family and home, the work involved may well be full-time in itself; entry into paid employment as well, even on a part-time basis, is more than most men do, and more than can be expected of an individual.

Nevertheless, it is instructive to know the reasons for having part-time work: of the 1,290,000 women who held part-time jobs in 1986, 12.5 per cent (161,000) did so because of "personal or family responsibilities" (other than children); 20.3 per cent (262,000) were "going to school"; 27.4 per cent (353,000) "could only find part-time work"; and 38.5 per cent (497,000) did not want full-time work. It is relevant to note that 86 per cent of those who did not want full-time work were married, which means they had family and home responsibilities. This is hardly the profile of a population that "prefers" part-time employment, when in fact more than one-quarter would rather have full-time employment and the rest have responsibilities that preclude the taking of full-time work.

Another argument against the preference thesis is the preference of employers. The assertion that many women are employed part-time because they prefer part-time work implicitly assumes that employers created part-time work to accommodate the preferences of women. In fact, many women are in part-time work because employers prefer to have them work part-time. Part-time employment is less costly to employers and provides greater flexibility in the scheduling of work than full-time employment, particularly in work activities which experience peaks and troughs during the work day and work activities that extend over periods of 10-12 hours per day, six or seven days per week, as in urban transport, airline ticket offices, retail trade, postal services, health services, and so on. Recent labour-management conflicts in the airlines and Canada Post were largely on this issue – a manifested preference by management for more part-time employees.

Another misconception about part-time work is the tendency to regard it as casual work. Such is not the case, of course: most part-time employment is continuing employment, scheduled by employers in the same way as full-time employment, and fitted by employees within their time schedules to accommodate their other responsibilities.

The fourth myth is that equal pay between men and women can be brought about without a radical social transformation in the role of women in the family and in the larger society. The elimination of inequality of opportunity and inequality in pay between men and women as well as among men and among women is a laudatory objective. But the provision of equal opportunity and the payment of equal wages for work of equal value are both predicated on more than a recognition that unequal opportunity is unfair and inefficient and that the payment of unequal wages is inequitable. Rather, a change is needed in cultural values, in attitudes, in behaviour. As long as women bear the primary responsibility for home and family they will continue to be regarded as secondary workers in the labour market, on the premise at least that it is not humanly possible to hold two full-time jobs and be efficient in both of them. This perception and the negative expectations associated with it can be ameliorated somewhat by the more widespread introduction of reputable day-care establishments and domestic services. Full equality between men and women and the associated equality of opportunity in employment will not come into effect until women and men are perceived as equals in relation to home and family responsibilities – when schools telephone fathers at work as readily as they telephone mothers when Johnny or Patsy is in trouble; when fathers stay home as readily as mothers do when the child has a fever; when mother packs her bags as readily as father does when employment responsibilities dictate travel, and the family accepts the event as readily as it does when father does it.

As long as women are perceived to have full responsibility for home and family, they will not be perceived equal to men in employment opportunities and pay. In such a context, legislation for equal pay for work of equal value will impact negatively on the employment of women. This is attested by the experience of Australia, where such legislation has been in effect since the early 1970s. As federal and state tribunals began to enforce the legislation by setting the same pay for all jobs judged to be comparable in skill, responsibility, effort, and working conditions, the rate of growth in women's employment began to suffer relative to that of men.[3]

Sociologists and anthropologists have identified a number of other myths about work and the role of women in society. Some of these are:

1. *The sexualization of work.* The world of work is largely a man's world. To the extent that women enter that world, they enter in subordinate roles, and they are at risk.
2. *The male breadwinner.* Man is responsible for the material well-being of the family. Women and children are dependants.
3. *The imitation syndrome.* Career women need male characteristics and male deportment to survive and succeed in man's world.
4. *The teleological shibboleth.* Since many women intend to marry, and many regard marriage and family a major vocation, they are necessarily vague and indifferent about vocational preparation and the nature of initial employment.[4]

A Profile of the Female Population

In 1981, women represented 50.4 per cent of the Canadian population (Table 2.1).

The majority (60 per cent) of women 15 years of age and over were living in husband-wife families, 6.3 per cent were heads of lone-parent families, 15.7 per cent were children living with their families, and 18 per cent were independent (not living with their families). More women (987,490) than men (693,640) were living alone. Among the husband-wife families, 56.9 per cent had children in the family; among the lone parents, 33.3 per cent were widows, 29.3 per cent had husbands who were absent (including separations), 26.4 per cent were divorced, and 11 per cent were single (never married). Marriage rates of women have declined steadily over time, while divorce rates have steadily increased (Table 2.2). The implication of this for the employment of women is that increasing numbers find it necessary to enter the labour market and remain in the labour market as long as their circumstances dictate.

Table 2.1

Female-Male Composition of the Canadian Population, 1981

Age Group	Women (000's)	Men (000's)	Total	Women as % of Total
0-14	2,669.9	2,811.0	5,480.9	48.7
15-24	2,302.4	2,356.3	4,658.7	49.4
25-34	2,110.3	2,105.9	4,216.2	50.1
35-44	1,471.2	1,497.0	2,968.2	49.6
45-54	1,242.4	1,256.4	2,498.8	49.7
55-64	1,128.4	1,030.8	2,159.2	52.3
65-74	806.0	671.8	1,477.8	54.5
75-Over	544.2	339.0	883.2	61.6
Total	12,274.9	12,068.3	24,343.2	50.4

SOURCE: Statistics Canada, *Women in Canada: A Statistical Report* (Ottawa: Supply and Services Canada, 1985), p. xvi, Table 2.

Participation in the Labour Force

The information indicates that a large and increasing proportion of women are not in husband-wife family relationships, and a significant proportion of these women have children. This is an important determining variable accounting for the increasing participation of women in paid labour market activity. In the absence of the traditional reliance on husband support, the alternative would be public support through social assistance. Most women in our society have as much pride in themselves as men do: they would rather work than depend on social assistance.

The participation of single women 15 years of age and over in paid employment has increased from 59.2 per cent in 1975 to 66.1 per cent in 1986; that of married women increased from 41.6 per cent to 56.1 per cent (Table 2.3). Women with dependent children have entered the labour force in increasing proportions: in 1975, 41.6 per cent of women with children under 16 years of age were in the labour force; in 1986, the proportion stood at 63.4 per cent. It is highly significant to future trends that the participation rates of women with very young children have increased substantially: 56 per cent of women with children of less than three years of age participated in 1986, compared with 31.2 per cent in 1975; 61.6 per cent of those with children in the 3-5 years age group; and 68.3 per cent of those with children 6-15 years of age.

Table 2.2

Marriage and Divorce Rates of Women, 1970-82

	Marriage Rates*	Divorce Rates**
1970	69.5	6.21
1971	69.2	6.07
1972	70.6	6.49
1973	68.3	7.20
1974	66.3	8.60
1975	64.1	9.42
1976	61.0	9.86
1977	57.4	9.89
1978	55.3	10.04
1979	54.5	10.29
1980	54.0	10.54
1981	52.6	11.29
1982	50.7	11.64

* Marriages per 1,000 single, widowed, and divorced population aged 15 years and over.

** Divorces per 1,000 married women aged 15 years and over.

SOURCE: Statistics Canada, *Women in Canada: A Statistical Report* (Ottawa: Supply and Services Canada, 1985), p. 10, Tables 8, 9.

Accounting for Increase in Participation

The steadily rising participation in the labour market by women of all ages, married and single, with and without children, has been attributed to a number of developments. Women are having *fewer children*: in 1970 the general fertility rate (which is the total number of live births per 1,000 women 15-49 years of age) was 71.2; by 1982 it fell to 56.3.[5] *Day-care facilities* and services have expanded considerably: in 1973 there were only 28,373 day-care spaces; in 1982 there were 123,962.[6] This is still grossly inadequate, but it is an improvement nevertheless. Women have been *postponing the bearing of children*: the median age of first childbirth has increased from 22.8 in 1971 to 24.6 in 1982.[7] On the average, women are earning *higher educational qualifications*, and there is a close correlation between the level of educational attainment and participation in the labour market: only 25.2

Table 2.3

Labour Force Participation of Women, 1975-86

	All Women 15 years and Over	Single Women	Married Women	With Dependent Children		
				Less than 3 Years	3-5 Years	6-15 Years
1975	44.4	59.2	41.6	31.2	40.0	48.2
1976	45.2	58.8	42.8	31.7	40.9	50.0
1977	46.0	59.0	44.2	34.0	42.5	51.9
1978	47.9	60.5	46.3	37.6	46.1	54.3
1979	49.0	61.8	47.5	39.4	47.8	55.6
1980	50.4	63.3	49.0	41.7	50.1	58.2
1981	51.7	64.6	50.6	44.5	52.4	61.1
1982	51.7	63.3	51.2	45.6	53.2	61.6
1983	52.6	64.0	52.3	48.9	55.6	62.0
1984	53.5	64.7	53.7	51.5	56.9	64.4
1985	54.3	65.7	54.7	53.9	59.6	66.2
1986	55.1	66.1	56.1	56.0	61.6	68.3

SOURCE: Statistics Canada, *Women in Canada: A Statistical Report* (Ottawa: Supply and Services Canada, 1985), pp. 17-18, Tables 18, 19, p. 48, Table 2, Statistics Canada, *The Labour Force*, December, 1984, 1985, and 1986.

per cent of women with less than Grade Nine education participated in the labour market in 1986, compared with 55.9 per cent of those with high school education, 67.2 per cent with some post-secondary education, 70.9 per cent with post-secondary certificate or diploma, and 78 per cent with university degrees.[8]

In 1971, 25,450 women earned Bachelor's degrees and first professional (medical, dental, engineering, law) degrees, 2,116 earned Master's degrees, and 151 earned doctoral degrees; in 1982, 44,397 earned Bachelor's and first professional degrees, 5,290 earned Master's degrees, and 423 earned doctoral degrees – a significant improvement in numbers within the relatively short period of one decade.

Also significant from the standpoint of participation in the labour market is the notable change in the distribution of the fields of study in which women enter. There is a decrease of concentration in the traditional fields of education, humanities, and general studies. Concurrently, a shift occurred to the more marketable fields of commerce, law, economics, and so on. For example, in 1971 close to 32 per cent of the Bachelor's degrees earned by women were in the field of education; 16.3 per cent were in humanities, and 17.5 per cent were general degrees.[9]

In 1982, the number earning education degrees decreased to 25.5 per cent of the total, the number in humanities fell to 12 per cent, and the number in general studies dropped to 10 per cent. This quest for marketable fields of study is evident also in graduate studies: the proportion of Master's degrees in humanities decreased from 35 per cent in 1971 to 20 per cent in 1982, whereas the proportion in commerce increased from 0.7 per cent to 10.4 per cent and those in education increased to 28.4 per cent from 18.7 per cent, undoubtedly in quest of administrative positions within the education system, which have been largely a male preserve.[10]

Other commonly cited factors responsible for the steadily increasing participation by women in the labour market is the *change in social attitudes*, both in relation to work-force participation *per se* and in relation to participation in specific occupations. Society no longer regards negatively the participation of women in work outside the home for pay, and although there may continue to exist some reluctance to approve without reservation their participation in all forms of employment activity – underground coal mining, flying fighter planes, working the night shift in a factory, bricklaying – the trend toward social indifference is evident.

Another major factor has been the *increase in employment opportunities for women*. This is the "demand-induced" thesis of participation, which postulates that increasing numbers of women were induced to enter market employment by the increase in employment opportunities suitable to their qualifications and preferences. In the absence of increases in employment opportunities in work people wish to perform, increasing participation results in unemployment. Indeed, it is often the case that participation is a response to increasing employment opportunities, particularly among women with young children whose economic circumstances do not dictate work for income, retired people who do not need to work for money, and young people. Therefore, participation for certain groups in society is both a response to the existence of employment opportunities and a stimulus to the creation of employment opportunities, as when, for example, a woman decides to open a shop, to offer day-care services, to provide typing services at home.

There was a saying, still valid for some women, that "a woman's work is never done." Indications now are that for most women the work that is related to home and family is not adequate, in quantity and nature, to be considered full-time work. Quite apart from the benefits of additional family income, the volume of work appears to have been reduced by the *increasing use of technology in work activities in the home* – machines washing and drying clothes and dishes, all sorts of cleaners, mechanical dusters, and vacuuming devices, microwave ovens – and the *increasing use of factory-prepared foods* – packaged, canned, frozen vegetables, mixes, cakes, cookies, dinners, cooked meats, etc. All of these have reduced the demand for work in the household economy, which means that the supply of labour that was allocated to the performance of such work is now available for employment in the external labour market. Furthermore, *wages in the external labour market have increased* progressively over time, increasing the opportunity cost of work in the household economy. For increasing numbers of women the cost of household work, in the form of forgone income, came to exceed the implicit value of the household work. Some women have elected to bear the difference in cost and remain within the household economy. But participation rates indicate that an increasing proportion of women 15 years of age and over have elected to take the income offered by the external market and use it to purchase some of the household work, such as day-care, entertainment, prepared foods, cleaning, laundering, and the like.

In the search for explanations for the dramatic increase in the participation of women in the labour market, it is common to emphasize such supply-side variables as the mechanization of the home, more work-related education, smaller families, and postponements in marriage and having children. Demand-side variables are not equally emphasized; yet, many of the supply-side variables may well be a response to developments on the demand side, *induced* and *facilitated* by increasing employment opportunities. This proposition finds support in the evidence that the most dramatic increase in the participation rates of women has coincided with the increase in government services (federal, provincial, and municipal), educational services, health and health-related services, and personal and community services. In other words, postponement of marriage and family, smaller families, more work-related education, and the mechanization of the home *made it possible* for women to enter and remain in the labour market; but the decision to enter was induced by the increasing availability of desirable employment opportunities at levels of pay that more than offset the costs (both implicit and explicit) associated with the decision to enter and stay in the labour market.

Such demand-induced participation and accommodative education and training responses involve a higher degree of commitment to employment than participation that does not involve any specific work-related preparation. *Investment in education and training* involves costs, in the form of direct expenditures and forgone employment earnings, which must be justified or recovered through employment. This is attested by the evidence of a consistent relationship over time between lifetime employment and levels of education and training. The more educated a woman, the more likely it is that she will be in the labour force, the more likely she will be in the labour force continuously, and the more likely she will remain in the labour force over a lifetime of work.[11] In addition to the "return to investment" explanation of this relationship, the nature of work bears on it, and so do the work environment, the prospects for advancement in employment and professional knowledge, and the positive effect of education and training on the productivity of labour market time relative to the productivity of time spent in the household. To the extent that education and training raise the productivity of time allocated to household activity, the cost of remaining in household production increases.[12]

This has significant implications for future participation rates, if the household economy expands the range of its production activities to the extent suggested by Jonathan Gershuny,[13] and if the household economy becomes linked to the commercial economy to the extent suggested by Alvin Toffler.[14] Gershuny's thesis is that microelectronic and telecommunications processes will expand the capacity for production in the home: just as washing machines, dryers, cleaners, mixers, freezers, and refrigerators expanded the production capacities of households, so computers, television transmission, recorders, and printers will expand that capacity further. In other words, microelectronic consumer durables will be used increasingly by households as producer goods, thereby shifting production activity from the commercial sector to the household sector. An increase in the production activities of households will, of course, provide increasing legitimacy to the argument for recognition of household work as employment work. Given such recognition, the participation rates of women will increase further. On the other hand, if work in the household economy remains unrecognized as employment, but the value of work in it increases to approximate the value in the market economy, participation rates motivated by differences in values between the household economy and the market economy may decline. Such a development will affirm Alvin Toffler's expectations of shifts in employment from the market economy to the household economy.

Toffler's observations relate to the historic dispersions of economic activity. He notes that in *the first wave* of economic and social development, work was dispersed "in the home, in the village, in the fields"; in *the second wave*, work became concentrated "in giant urban centres ... and in factories where thousands of labourers were drawn together under a single roof."[15] *The third wave* is ushering the onset of "smaller work units ... decentralization and de-urbanization of production," and the shift of jobs "out of the factories and offices into which the second wave swept them and right back where they came from originally: the home."[16]

To summarize the main factors responsible for the significant increase in the participation of women in the market economy: *on the supply side*, the increase in capital intensity of household activities, smaller families, and increasing levels of education reduced the relative value of work in the household economy, while *on the demand side*, increasing employment opportunities and rising wages increased the cost of staying in the household economy. As to the future, should it happen that as a result of new technologies high value-added work shifts from the market economy to the household economy, as suggested by Gershuny and Toffler, and the gap in value of work in the two economies narrows significantly, the trend to increasing participation in the market economy may indeed be arrested.

Participation and Reservation Wages

A theoretical explanation for the participation of women in paid work involves the relationship between the wages to be earned in the market economy and the value that is put to leisure and non-market work activities. The lower the value of leisure and the value of non-market work activities, the lower is likely to be the reservation wage, which is defined as the minimum wage that will induce people to offer their services in the marketplace. The lower the reservation wage, the lower will be the market wage necessary to induce participation in market work activity. Low reservation wage means that the person does not highly value the time spent at leisure and at non-market work activities. Conversely, the higher the value that people place on leisure and non-market work activities, the higher will be their reservation wages, and the higher would market wages need to be to induce them to offer their services in the market. People who enjoy the activities in which they engage after their market work will place a high value to their time after work, which will be reflected in their reservation wages for that time. When such people are given the opportunity to reduce the time allocated to market work, they will put a high reservation wage to that additional "free" time as well. For example, a mother with a dependent child will place a high value on her time with the child, which means that for different *blocks of time* (morning, afternoon, evening) she will have different reservation wages, ranging from competitive, which makes participation in market work activities possible, to noncompetitive, which effectively makes participation most unlikely.

Such an approach to the question of participation and nonparticipation in market work activities by women with dependent children provides the economic rationale in decisions. It means that women who withdraw from market work and stay out of the market during the early formative years of their children place a higher value to their work with the children than what they would have earned from outside employment. In instances where the market price is high and approaches or exceeds the value assigned to non-market work, as is often the case with women in professional and management occupations, withdrawals from the market are often limited to very brief periods preceding and following the birth of a child.

This development provides an important explanation for the rising trend in the participation of women over the past two decades and suggests perhaps a continuing upward trend: the levels of education of women have been rising generally and increasing numbers have been entering into professional and management occupations; in parallel, the value of market work has risen significantly over the past two decades. As a result, withdrawal from the market involves increasing sacrifice of income. The question arises whether the value assigned to non-market work, which is often rather subjective, has risen proportionately or more or less than proportionately. Also, if the matter were approached from the husband-wife perspective, the question of who should remain at home and who should stay in the market is answered implicitly: economic rationale would suggest that the person whose market value is the greater should remain in the market. It is conceivable, of course, that the market prices and the satisfaction derived from market work by both husband and wife are higher than the value assigned to non-market work and leisure, in which case the rational economic decision would be to vest responsibility for the non-market work, including child care, to others.

These comments suggest that reservation wages tend to change with changes in family circumstances: the addition of a child into the family will influence the reservation wages of the mother, the father, and other members of the family (working grandmother, for example, in many ethnic families).[17] The value of time spent at home tends to increase and may well exceed the value of time spent at market work. In such case, the rational decision would be to withdraw from the market. This is the economic explanation for the general tendency to change the employment status of some family members upon the addition of a child in the family, or when family circumstances so change as to increase the value of time spent at home relative to the value of time spent at work. The same reasoning enters, of course, when the value of time spent at work decreases relative to the value of time spent at home – wages decreasing, the work environment becoming increasingly depressing, or the work itself becoming unpleasant can reduce the value of market work below the value of non-market work and leisure. Many withdrawals from the market and changes in employment status from full-time to part-time can be explained by such changes in relative values.

Participation and Differences in Earnings

In the 1970s and early 1980s, the earnings of women averaged about 60 per cent those of men. But after adjustments for productivity-related characteristics (education, age, etc.) and for broad occupational and industrial distributions, the average increases to about 80 per cent. The differential narrows even further, to the 90 per cent range, for narrowly defined occupations within individual establishments.[18]

Studies of changes in the earnings gap indicate some narrowing has taken place over the 1970s.[19] That is quite remarkable in the context of the significant increase in the supply of women in the labour market over the indicated period. Between 1970 and 1986 the number of women in the labour force increased form 2,824,000 to 5,523,000, or by 2,699,000. This represents an average annual increase over the period of almost 169,000. By contrast, the number of men in the labour force increased from 5,571,000 to 7,347,000, for an average annual increase of 111,000 (see Table 2.4). Such a phenomenal increase in the supply of women in the labour market should, other things being equal, have an arresting effect on the rate of increase in their wages.

The recorded improvements in women/men pay differentials, in the context of the very substantial increase in the supply of women, mean a number of positive changes have taken place in the interim, among which the more important are: more women in higher-paid occupations; an increase in productivity-related characteristics of women (education and employment-related skills); a progressive increase in the duration of employment; and a general increase in de-

mand for women in employment.This last probably accounts for most
of the improvement: had demand for women in employment not increased at least proportionately to the increase in supply, the improvement in characteristics of women in employment, including the increase of women in higher-paid occupations, would not have sustained
and improved their relative pay positions.

Table 2.4
The Canadian Labour Force: Men/Women Mix, 1970-86

Year	Total Labour Force (000's)	Men	Women	Women as Per Cent of Total Labour Force
1970	8,395	5,571	2,824	33.6%
1971	8,639	5,667	2,972	34.4
1972	8,898	5,797	3,101	34.9
1973	9,276	5,973	3,303	35.6
1974	9,640	6,163	3,477	36.1
1975	9,974	6,294	3,680	36.9
1976	10,204	6,368	3,836	37.6
1977	10,501	6,505	3,996	38.1
1978	10,896	6,657	4,239	38.9
1979	11,231	6,811	4,420	39.4
1980	11,573	6,935	4,638	40.1
1981	11,904	7,053	4,851	40.8
1982	11,957	7,031	4,926	41.2
1983	12,182	7,098	5,084	41.7
1984	12,399	7,169	5,231	42.2
1985	12,639	7,257	5,382	42.6
1986	12,870	7,347	5,523	42.9

SOURCE: Statistics Canada, *Women in Canada*, p. 47; *The Labour Force*, December
1984, 1985, 1986.

Years of service with individual enterprises also appears to
bear on the subject: the theory of internal labour markets postulates
widespread horizontal and vertical mobility within enterprises over
time, with automatic adjustments in pay, and general improvements
in the terms and conditions of employment of individual employees
by virtue of "length of service." Men have had an advantage in this, but

evidence suggests women are closing the gap rapidly. In 1985, one in three men (34 per cent) had more than eleven years of job tenure, and one in eight (13 per cent) had more than twenty years; among women, one in five (20 per cent) had eleven years and over, and only one in twenty (5 per cent) had over twenty years. But a significant change is evident in individual occupations, which reflects the influx of women into the labour market in the past decade and into higher-level occupations and employments: in managerial and professional occupations, for example, only 5 per cent of the women had more than twenty years of tenure, while 14 per cent of the men had more than twenty years; but 20 per cent of the women had 11-20 years of tenure, which is not much different from the 25 per cent of the men; and 23 per cent of the women had 6-10 years of tenure, compared with 19 per cent of the men. Therefore, aside from the over-twenty-years group, where men predominate, the respective proportions of men and women in managerial and professional occupations with job tenure of 6-20 years have become almost equal – 43 per cent of women and 44 per cent of men.[20] This has important implications for the future for both men and women: to the extent that the length of job tenure has been an important criterion in promotions and pay, women are removing a significant deficiency from their employment résumés.

A report by the U.S. Bureau of the Census indicates that differences between men and women in work experience, in the number and length of work interruptions, and in the average level of education account for close to 15 per cent of the differences in earnings.[21] Considering the indicated trends in these variables, it can be reasonably expected that the pay differentials will continue to narrow.

Differences in Pay Among Occupations and Employments

Differences in pay among various occupations and within occupations should reflect the differences in contributions people make to the value of goods and services in whose production they participate. When we speak of discriminatory pay practices we mean that some people get paid more than their contribution to the value of goods and services they help to produce, while some other people get paid less than their contribution.[22]

There prevails a view in society at large, particularly among lower and middle-level occupations and employments, in which women predominate, that upper-level occupations and occupations holding central positions in production processes exploit their positions of advantage and gain for themselves pay in excess of their contributions. It is coincidental that such occupations commonly exercise control over their numbers, regulate the nature and range of services their members provide, and even dictate the nature and range of services provided by other occupations associated with them in production. Such controls and influences enable them to influence the value of their services relative to the values of the services of occupations related to them in production.

Consider, for example, the occupations that render health services, such as physicians, nurses, therapists, technicians, and pharmacists. Although all of them have some form of certification, they vary significantly in the degree of restrictiveness in the certification process and in the extent to which one can influence the range of work functions of the others. Only one of these occupations – physicians – has such powers, and there is widespread belief that doctors use their powers to benefit themselves at the expense of the other occupations that participate in the provision of health services. This equally applies, of course, to dentists, dental hygienists, dental technicians, and others involved in the provision of dental services; lawyers, para-legal occupations, and legal secretaries involved in the provision of legal services; accountants, bookkeepers, accounting clerks, and others involved in the provision of accounting services; and so on.

The perception of widespread inequities in payment relative to contributions is not limited to inter-occupational comparisons; they exist also within occupations. Rules and regulations on minimum academic qualifications, apprenticeship periods, certification and licensing, and evaluation procedures establish privileged groups within occupations that often gain at the expense of those who occupy junior positions. For example, the requirement by universities, and increasingly now by community colleges, of a Ph.D. degree for permanent appointments to academic positions means that people with Master's degrees are segregated into the lowest teaching ranks, given heavier teaching loads than the permanent staff, and paid substantially lower salaries, and their appointments are commonly limited to each academic session in turn. Such are the academic positions of many women in universities and colleges.

The distribution of employment incomes in Canada conveys the impression of widespread inequities. To the extent that the distribution is presumed to reflect contributions, then some people are attributed contributions and given payments that are considerably higher than what they should be, while many others are attributed contributions and given payments that are considerably lower than what they should be. If this perception reflects the reality, then the distribution of incomes from employment violates our society's sense of equity. This is what underlies the push for equal pay for work of equal value. There is a sense that the wages paid to women are lower than the wages paid to men not because women contribute less than men do, but because they are women. Society's sense of equity and fairness is being called to account.

But recognition that the pay structure is inequitable relative to contributions does not mean there is social consensus on what pay differences should be among occupations and employments.[23] The average citizen's concept of the relative worth of different occupations is influenced by all kinds of values and perceptions, including the influence of well-organized publicity by individual occupations. A good test of this would be to have a group of citizens *rank* the occupations listed in Table 2.5 in terms of what their incomes should be – 1 (highest), 2 (second highest), 3 (third highest), and so on; indicate what the amount of annual income for each should be; and provide *justification* for the suggested rankings and amounts of income. The outcome will be chaotic.

The absence of social consensus on what is an equitable wage and salary structure does not mean, of course, the public authority has no responsibility to ensure that citizens enjoy equitable treatment in employment and pay. It is incumbent on governments to identify and remove the sources of inequity and their inequitable outcomes. For example, should it be determined that some professions exploit to their advantage the self-regulating power bestowed on them, the legislation bestowing such powers can be amended to increase competition and/or reduce price-fixing arrangements that cause inequities. Similarly, if collective bargaining is responsible for inequities, a tax-based incomes policy[24] may have the necessary corrective effect. And, of course, if it were established that the inequities reflect sex biases, the equal-pay-for-equal-value criterion should be invoked.

Equity in employment and pay is a troublesome issue in all societies, regardless of their economic systems and social and political structures. The source of difficulty is that it involves value judgements based on philosophy, tradition, culture, and self-interest. Unlike decisions on economic efficiency, which involve the means used to obtain certain economic ends, equity decisions involve the distribution of the ends of the economy – who should get what.[25]

Advocates of market determination of employment and pay avoid the issue of equity by making reference to the operation of market forces: whatever the outcomes – segregation in employment, unemployment, inequitable distribution of income – they are attributed to

Table 2.5
Ranking Occupations by Employment Incomes:
What Should They Earn?

Occupations	Rank	Annual Income	Justifications
Lawyer			
High school teacher			
Secretary/typist			
Electrician			
Physician (general practice)			
Nurse			
Postal worker			
Accountant			
Bookkeeper			
Engineer			
Auto assembly worker			
President of large company			
Insurance salesman			
Member of Parliament			
Senior government bureaucrat			
Brewery worker			

demand and supply. It is assumed people choose freely the employments into which they enter, and therefore the outcomes reflect occupational choices, work and leisure choices, relative productivities, and other individual decisions that bear on who gets what, who is employed, and who is employed where.

The question is how free are free markets, and to what extent are occupational choices free expressions of peoples' preferences? To what extent are the observed market outcomes the result of competitive forces, and to what extent are they manifestations of discriminatory practices? What of those whose social and economic positions limit the range of their choices? What was the range of occupational choices of women who wanted to pursue professional careers twenty or so years ago, or a hundred years ago?

Market-determined distributions are not value-free: whatever their nature, they will reflect in part the values of the existing social and political systems, the status quo.[26] The relative values attached to the services of artists, physicians, electricians, accountants, teachers, and nurses, and the corresponding payments for their services, reflect market forces as well as a certain social perception of the relative values of those occupations in society. The question is, whose values are reflected in the "social" values? The historical record of employment discrimination and segregation may give women cause to conclude that the prevailing social values have reflected largely the teachings, practices, and biases of men.

It is important to emphasize that a quest for equity in employment and pay is not a quest for equality, except for equality of opportunity and equal treatment of equals. In other words, the issue is not whether differential prizes should exist, or whether people should be allocated to work in accordance with their qualifications, assessed potential, and experience. The issue, rather, is whether the differential prizes reflect relative contributions and whether the allocations to employment reflect qualifications, unbiased assessments of potential, and unbiased evaluations of experience. Our employment structure and distributive system are burdened with value judgements that, over time, have resulted in serious inequities in employment and pay,[27] particularly as they relate to the employment and pay of women.

The principle of equal pay for work of equal value seems to respond to this problem. It is founded on the long-recognized rationale in economics that equity in pay must be based on relative contributions to the value of output. The problem has been in the difficulty of measuring relative contributions, particularly in services and activities that constitute a fraction of the market value of final products. How does one determine, for example, the contribution of an office worker employed by an automobile manufacturer to the value of an automobile? This difficulty gives an advantage to those who have gained strong competitive positions in the marketplace and those who occupy key positions in processes of production. Such workers gain at the expense of those whose positions in the market are relatively weak and those whose positions in the work process are remote and subordinated.

The principle of equal pay for work of equal value seeks to overcome this difficulty by shifting the focus away from relative contributions to output and to (1) the *activities* in which people are engaged, (2) the *skills* required for those activities, (3) the *effort* people put into the work, (4) the *responsibilities* they bear in their work, and (5) the *envi-*

ronment in which they carry out their work activities. It is implicitly assumed that the composite of these qualifications and work-related characteristics will reflect the value of contributions made to output.

The establishment of equitable standards of comparability is no less difficult, of course, than the measurement of relative contributions to output by different occupations involved in the production of individual products and services.[28] We turn our attention now to an examination of equal pay for work of equal value.

Equal Pay for Work of Equal Value

Unlike legislation that invokes the principle of *equal pay for equal work* for people generally who are employed at jobs that are identical or similar in the work functions they perform, legislation that calls for *equal pay for work of equal value* focuses on the principle of equal pay for work that is determined to be of the same value regardless of the nature of the work.[29] It provides for the assignment of values to individual jobs on the basis of the skills involved in the work, the effort required, the responsibilities entailed, and the working environment in which the job is performed. The composite value of these four job characteristics would constitute the comparative value of the work.

This is a radical departure from the determination of job values in market economies, where demand and supply are the determinants, with demand reflecting the contributions individuals make to the value of the output of the goods and services they produce, and supply reflecting the number of people with the required qualifications and experience available for the production of that output of goods and services. The system of equal pay for work of equal value assumes implicitly that contributions to the value of output are reflected or should be reflected in the skills, effort, and responsibilities, and that the nature of the working environment is a relevant factor as well. The supply side is neutralized, which is a common development in occupations where pay is negotiated through collective bargaining. Although we like to think that the supply of people with qualifications to be automobile workers, postal workers, or brewery workers bears on their wages, in reality the employment contracts setting the pay of those workers neutralize the pay and other terms and conditions of employment from developments in the external market for the duration of the contract (and, experience would suggest, for the long run), barring very significant permanent changes in the nature of outputs and organization of the processes in which the workers are involved. Such is not the case, of course, when workers are not organized; then, the pay and other terms and conditions of employment are not determined by collective bargaining. In such non-unionized sectors of the economy, the supply of people in the market at large does influence the pay, which is the chief motivation for legislation on equal pay for work of equal value, since most sectors in which women are employed fall into this category.

Differences in earnings of men and women are given in Table 2. 6, in the form of adjusted and unadjusted ratios. The adjusted ratios reflect adjustments for differences in productivity-related variables, such as education, experience, and broad occupational groups.

All studies indicate that the earnings of women in full-time, full-year employment have averaged on the aggregate (all establishments, occupations, industries, and regions) at about 60 per cent of the earnings of men. When adjusted for differences in productivity-related variables, such as education, experience, and broad occupational groups, the average increases to 80 per cent, which means the differential in favour of men decreases from 40 per cent to 20 per cent. When comparisons are limited to narrowly defined occupations adjusted for the productivity-related variables (education and experience), the average increases to 90-95 per cent, which means the deficiency in the earnings of women compared to those of men decreases to 5-10 per cent.

The difference in the earnings gap between the average of all occupational groups and the narrowly defined occupations suggests that more than half of the difference may be accounted for by differences in occupational concentrations – more women than men are concentrated in low-paying occupations and employments. Also, the 5-10 per cent difference within narrowly defined occupations may be explained by the concentration of women at the lower levels of individual occupations. This suggests, in turn, that the indicated differences in average earnings, whether in the economy at large, in broad occupational groups, or in individual occupations may be more the result of occupational choices and occupational segregation than the result of pay discrimination. If such is the case, then the application of equal pay for work of equal value will not have much effect on the difference in average earnings between men and women.

Some of the inequities will undoubtedly be reduced or even removed, but differences in average earnings will remain as long as women remain concentrated in low-paying occupations and as long as they remain largely concentrated at the lower levels of individual high-paid occupations. Such concentrations not only pull down the average earnings of women, but also, and much more importantly, underuti-

Table 2.6

Female/Male Earnings Ratio, Unadjusted and Adjusted for Various Productivity-Related Factors in Various Canadian Studies

Study	Year and Data	Gross Unadjusted Ratio	Net Adjusted Ratio
Ostry (1968)	1961 Census	0.59	0.81
Robson and Lapointe (1971)	University faculty 1965/66	0.80	0.90
Gunderson (1975)	Narrowly defined occupation same establ., 1968/69	0.82	0.93
Shrank (1977)	University faculty 1973/74	0.83	0.95
Robb (1978)	1971 Census, Ontario males cf. single females over 30	0.60 n.a.	0.76 0.94
Gunderson (1979)	1971 Census	0.60	0.77
Stelcner (1979)	University faculty 1976/77	0.91	0.94
Walmsley et al. (1980)	Sask. organization, 1980	0.80	0.87
Gunderson (1980)	1971 Census, Ontario	0.60	0.76
Shapiro and Stelcner (1980)	1971 Census Canada public Canada private Quebec public Quebec private	0.65 0.57 0.66 0.56	0.83 0.72 0.87 0.74
Stelcner and Shapiro (1980)	1971 Census, Quebec, single over 30	0.60 0.83	0.82 0.82
Kapsalis (1980)	1975 Survey of Cons. Finance	0.61	0.87

SOURCE: Morley Gunderson, "Discrimination, Equal Pay and Equal Opportunities in the Labour Market," in *Work and Pay: The Canadian Labour Market*, Vol. 17, research studies prepared for the Royal Commission on the Economic Union and Development Prospects for Canada (Toronto: University of Toronto Press, 1985).

lize the productive capacities of women, which influences their pay. The fact is that aside from pay discrimination, differences in pay are accounted for by differences in *actual* and *potential* contributions to the activities in which enterprises (commercial, industrial, and institutional) are engaged. *Actual* contributions are a function of education, experience, intelligence, and the nature of activities in which the individual is engaged; *potential* contributions are a function of evaluations of the individual's capacity to assume increasing responsibilities.

Women are held back in relation to both actual and potential contributions: their actual contributions are constrained by the nature of work activities assigned to them, which often are of lower level and lower value than the activities assigned to men with the same and even lower education, experience, and intelligence; their potential contributions are reduced by the limited opportunities they have to gain the wide-ranging work experience regarded important for elevation to the higher levels of the employment structure.

Equal pay for work of equal value looks at the jobs men and women do, not at what they can do. It does not look at the critical question: why are men and women with the same qualifications assigned different work responsibilities, which then influence their current pay and their potential earnings? In a free competitive working environment, differences in earnings among people with the same educational qualifications reflect differences in innate abilities, in experience, in opportunity to contribute, in consistency of contributions over time, in reliability, in co-operation with other employees, in willingness to undertake responsibilities. These and many other factors comprise the composite of the working person within an organization of working people, co-operating and competing with one another, supplementing each other's work, complementing or impeding one another's work, some doing the best they can, others performing below their capacities and affecting the capacities of others. These differences and characteristics will be reflected in differences of earnings between men and women, among men, and among women. The critical question is whether all workers are given equal opportunity to compete for the assignments that will bring the highest returns.

Notes

1. N. Swords-Isherwood *et al.*, "Technical Change and Its Effects on Employment Opportunities for Women," in P. Marstrand, ed., *New Technology and the Future of Work and Skills* (London: Frances Pinter, 1984), pp. 191-213.
2. All statistical information is from Statistics Canada, *The Labour Force*, Cat. no. 71-001, December, 1986.
3. R.G. Gregory and R.C. Duncan, "Segmented Labour Market Theories and the Australian Experience of Equal Pay for Women," *Journal of Post-Keynesian Economics* (1981), pp. 403-28.

4. Judith Long Laws, "Work Aspiration of Women: False Leads and New Starts," in Martha Blaxall and Barbara Reagan, *Women and the Workplace* (Chicago: University of Chicago Press, 1976), pp. 33-49.
5. Statistics Canada, *Vital Statistics*, Cat. nos. 84-202, 84-204.
6. National Health and Welfare, *Day Care Spaces in Canada, 1982.*
7. Statistics Canada, *Vital Statistics*, Cat. nos. 84-001, 84-204.
8. Statistics Canada, *Labour Force Annual Averages, 1975-1983* Cat. no. 71-529; *The Labour Force*, December, 1986.
9. Statistics Canada, *Women in Canada: A Statistical Report*, Cat. no. 89-503E, p. 31, Table 4.
10. *Ibid*, p. 32, Table 5.
11. Glen G. Cain, *Married Women in the Labour Force* (Chicago: University of Chicago Press, 1966); W.G. Bowen and T.A. Finegan, *The Economics of Labor Force Participation* (Princeton, N.J.: Princeton University Press, 1969); Jacob Mincer, "Labor Force Participation of Married Women: A Study of Labor Supply," in National Bureau of Economic Research, *Aspects of Labor Economics* (Princeton, N.J.: Princeton University Press, 1962).
12. Arleen Leibowitz, "Education and Home Production," *American Economic Review* (May, 1974), pp. 243-50.
13. Jonathan Gershuny, *After Industrial Society: The Emerging Self-Service Economy* (London: Macmillan, 1978).
14. Alvin Toffler, *The Third Wave* (New York: Bantam Books, 1980).
15. *Ibid.*, p. 53.
16. *Ibid.*, p. 194.
17. Daniel S. Hamermesh and Albert Rees examine this issue in considerable detail in *Economics of Work and Pay*, third edition (New York: Harper & Row, 1984), pp. 8-10.
18. Morley Gunderson presents a summary table of the findings of investigators in "Discrimination, Equal Pay, and Equal Opportunities in the Labour Market," in W. Craig Riddell, *Work and Pay: The Canadian Labour Market*, Study No. 17, Royal Commission on the Economic Union and Development Prospects for Canada (Toronto: University of Toronto Press, 1985), pp. 219-65.
19. *Ibid.*, p. 234.
20. The statistical information on job tenure is from Statistics Canada, *The Labour Force*, Cat. no. 71-001, December, 1985.
21. U.S. Bureau of the Census, "Lifetime Work Experience and Its Effect on Earnings: Retrospective Data From the 1979 Income Survey Development Program," *Current Population Reports*, Series P 23, No. 136 (Washington, D.C.: Government Printing Of-

fice, 1985).

22. This issue is examined in considerable detail by Lester C. Thurow in *Generating Inequality: Mechanisms on Distribution in the U.S. Economy* (New York: Basic Books, 1975); and in *The Zero-Sum Society: Distribution and Possibilities for Economic Change* (New York: Basic Books, 1980).

23. Dan Usher discusses this issue and its implications for income policies in *The Economic Prerequisite for Democracy* (London: Basil Blackwell, 1981). The comments that follow are from my *Issues in Management-Labour Relations in the 1990s* (London: Macmillan, 1985), pp. 54-56.

24. H. Wallich and S. Weintraub have proposed such a policy as an anti-inflationary measure in "A Tax-Based Incomes Policy," *Journal of Economic Issues* (June, 1971), pp. 1-19.

25. A very creditable examination of the issue will be found in Thurow's *Generating Inequality*.

26. *Ibid.*, p. 22.

27. See *ibid.*; John Rawls, *A Theory of Justice* (Cambridge, Mass.: Harvard University Press, 1971); Usher, *Economic Prerequisite*; George Gilder, *Wealth and Poverty* (New York: Basic Books, 1981).

28. Problems with the subject matter are examined in four articles in the *Monthly Labor Review* (December, 1985).

29. Roberta Edgecombe Robb, "Equal Pay for Work of Equal Value: Issues and Policies," *Canadian Public Policy* (December, 1987), pp. 445-61.

3

Occupational Discrimination

Why are women underrepresented in some occupations? Why have some occupations become "non-traditional" for women? A number of reasons have been suggested:

1. *The perpetuation of gender-based stereotyping of occupations,* such as surgeon, plumber, truck driver, secretary-typist, receptionist, cashier;

2. *The notion that women have primary responsibility for home and family* and therefore cannot be employed and assigned responsibilities that involve travel and work beyond regular working hours;

3. *Incompatibility between primary responsibility for home and family and commitment to work responsibility.* Anecdotal evidence is found to support the contention that in conflicts between family needs and work, family needs tend to prevail, particularly when the family needs involve children;

4. *Gender-based stereotyping has resulted in consumer expectations and preferences of one sex over the other.* Expectations and preferences result in the association of the traditional with competence, efficiency, and quality. The profit-maximizing employer will discriminate among potential employees in accordance with demonstrated consumer preferences. If consumers regard women lawyers, for example, less effective in courtroom proceedings than men and refuse to pay the standard legal fee for such services when provided by women, law firms will be reluctant to employ women lawyers in courtroom proceedings. As long as consumer

preferences remain biased, women lawyers will be assigned to activities toward which consumers are gender-indifferent.[1]

These reasons suggest that the underrepresentation of women in some occupations is founded on long-standing practice, which evolved into the association of occupations with the dominant gender group that provided the occupational services – surgeon/man, nurse/woman; chef/man, dietician/woman; engineer/man, cashier/woman; bricklayer/man, secretary/woman.

We know that work activities characterized as "women's work" have been so characterized because they have been performed largely by women. In years past, men-servants were as common as women-servants; men clerks were more common than women clerks; and there were more men bank tellers than women. Aside from the need for physical strength for certain jobs, there is nothing in the range of the work functions of different jobs that would make them more suitable for women than for men or vice versa.

The typecasting of jobs as "men's job" and "women's job" will continue as long as women predominate in some jobs and men predominate in others. If such typecasting is to be phased out, and if newly emerging occupations and employments are to be sex-neutral, men and women must be given *equal opportunity* to enter into them from the outset, and men and women must be allowed to function in their jobs together. This is particularly important in newly emerging occupations that have not established a sex identity. Yet, this is not what has happened in computer-related employments: at the outset men became directors and managers, systems analysts and programmers, while women became keypunch operators, data entry operators, tape librarians, scheduling clerks, and accounts clerks. As a result, the occupations of systems analyst and programmer assumed male connotations, whereas the occupations of data entry and data control, for example, assumed female connotations.

Such association of men and women with certain activities within newly emerging occupational structures will perpetuate the division of jobs into those for men and those for women. Equal opportunity to entry and employment in long-established occupations will not bring about significant changes in the foreseeable future. The numbers involved for replacements and additions to the total of workers in occupations are usually relatively small. As a result, even significant changes in the sex composition of the replacements and additions will not change significantly the largely male or largely female composition of the total occupational work force. Consider, for example, the present gender composition of physicians and lawyers: the very substantial change in the male/female mix of new entrants into the two professions over the past two decades has not changed significantly the mix of the total stock. This is why the emphasis is put on equal opportunity to employment in emerging occupations and employments.

Occupational Segregation

Four types of occupational segregation can be identified.[2] The first is *horizontal segregation*, where individual occupations are identified with and are dominated by women or men – clerical and secretarial work, nursing, kindergarten and elementary school teaching, and retail sales are identified with women and dominated by women, while electricians and plumbers, garbage collectors, bricklayers, carpenters and painters, engineers and business managers are identified with and dominated by men. The legal, medical, and accounting professions are also identified with and dominated by men, but that is changing to such an extent that sex identification is gradually fading away.

The second form of occupational segregation is *vertical segregation*. This manifests itself in the fewer and fewer women as one moves up the hierarchy of employment. An examination of the employment stratification of individual occupations and employments will establish that women progress with reasonable degrees of success up to the middle levels of the managerial and occupational infrastructure, but thereafter their progress slows down very significantly, even in occupations dominated by women.

The third form of occupational segregation is a *pseudo horizontal and vertical segregation*, which manifests itself in the creation of additional middle management positions horizontally in lieu of elevation to higher-level positions – a sort of consolation prize for failure to promote.

The fourth form of occupational segregation is *intra-occupational segregation*, which manifests itself in segregation *within* occupations in relation to special assignments, appointments to important committees, and the like. Such assignments and appointments often are the first step in the promotion screening process. Intra-occupational segregation in the assignment of functional responsibilities is the most critical form of segregation, since it determines who will be given the opportunity to gain experience and demonstrate the necessary qualities for higher and broader responsibilities, that is, promotion.

The reasons for segregation vary widely, from employment to employment, occupation to occupation, and individual to individual. Tradition and prejudice enter into the decision-making process, and there are instances in which segregation is a manifestation of employee preferences. It is possible, of course, that when women choose to enter employments known to be crowded and relatively low paid, they do so because the range of choices available to them is limited. But is the argument of a "limited range of choices" an adequate explanation? Is it not possible that they enter into some crowded occupations because they expect greater satisfaction from the work and the work environment in them than from the alternatives available to them for the same investment in education and training? The majority of women (and men) have high school education or less. What types of employment are superior alternatives to clerical positions for a high school graduate? What employment positions dominated by men with high school education or less would women prefer to the office and retail trade employments into which they are "segregated"? The negative connotation of "crowding" and "segregation" may, in fact, convey an inaccurate impression of the rationale underlying the choices women make from among the alternatives available to them, given the qualifications they offer. Relative pay may not be a primary consideration. The nature of work, the work environment, work relationships, flexibility and variety of work, transferability of the work experience, and such other considerations all enter into the decision-making process.[3]

Jobs and Women's Jobs

What is in a job that would make it a woman's job? Do jobs have any specific characteristics in their functional activities, or in the ways the work is organized, or in the ways they are scheduled that would make them more appropriate for women than for men? Do women have any specific aptitudes, not found in men, that would make them the rational choices for some types of work activity? Do they have any special aptitudes for interpersonal communication? Are they more empathetic than men? Are women more emotional? More submissive? Are they by nature more subservient than men? Do they have lesser aptitude for scientific and technical work?

All these, and many other questions, enter into the discussions of the almost universal concentration of women into different occupational groups than those into which men have tended to concentrate. Notwithstanding differences in educational systems among nations, in cultures and customs, in levels of economic and social development, and in political systems, men and women will be found largely segregated in employment into non-competing groups. The proportions of women in individual occupations may vary from country to country, but in the overall distribution women and men tend to be concentrated in different occupational groups. For example, a larger proportion of physicians and engineers are women in the Soviet Union than in Canada, but a larger proportion of accountants and a smaller proportion of street cleaners are women in Canada than in the Soviet Union. Nevertheless, an examination of the overall occupational distribution will establish that in both countries women predominate in secretarial and clerical employments, in retail trade, in nursing and teaching, in hotel and catering services, etc. In 1984, about 70 per cent of men and women in paid employment were in service activities, including services related to the production of goods. About half of the men and women employed in service activities were involved in office work, and about 70 per cent of all employees in offices were women. Clearly, service activities in general and office activities in particular are very significant sources of employment for women.

The experiences of women as workers in the labour market are common the world over, regardless of political systems. Differences do exist, but the characteristics common to all in employment are more revealing of the true positions of women in the world of work than are the distinctive characteristics. One common characteristic is the very limited number of women in high-level political positions, even in countries where the highest political positions have been occupied by women, such as Britain under Thatcher, India under Indira Gandhi, and Israel under Golda Meir.

In the Soviet Union, whose constitution proclaims full equality between men and women in all respects, few women will be found in high-level governing bodies in industry, institutions, professional groups, and governments. Even in those professional occupations in which women predominate, such as medicine, few women are found among academicians, directors, and high-level specialists. In the government itself, in 1985 there were no women in the highest governing body of the nation – the politburo; there were no women in the cabinet; there were only twelve women in the Central Committee of the Soviet Communist Party, which is constituted of 307 members; and there were only four women among the 170 candidate members of the Central Committee, the pool from which the new members of the Central Committee are drawn.[4]

Another common characteristic in the employment of women the world over is the relatively small numbers in senior bureaucratic positions at all levels of government – municipal, state, central – in all countries. Women outnumber men in public-sector employment, yet men outnumber women by far in management-level bureaucratic positions. In boards and commissions, agencies and institutes, which in most countries constitute a very significant part of public administration, few women will be found in senior positions. The same is true in public and private commercial enterprises.

Women in the Corporate World

In 1985, the chief executive officers of the top 500 companies in Canada were all men. And the boards of directors of all major corporations were made up almost entirely of men.

Table 3.1
Women on Boards of Directors of Major Corporations in Canada, 1986-87

	Board of Directors		
Company	Total	Men	Women
Canadian Pacific Ltd.	22	21	1
Southam Inc.	17	16	1
Bell Canada Enterprises	20	18	2
Canada Trust (CT Financial Services Inc.)	35	34	1
Canadian Utilities Ltd.	16	16	0
Gulf Canada Ltd.	18	17	1
Noranda	19	19	0
TransAlta Utilities	14	14	0
Nova-An Alberta Corporation	15	15	0
Hudson's Bay Company	15	14	1
Petro-Canada	15	13	2
Imperial Oil Ltd.	10	9	1
Royal Bank of Canada	44	42	2
Bank of Nova Scotia	31	29	2

SOURCE: Annual reports.

Boards of directors are policy-making bodies – on development of products and markets, on developments of human resources, on new undertakings, on financial policies. It is logical, then, that the composition of the board of directors of each company should reflect the relative importance of the respective policy objectives. With this in mind, one would be hard pressed to find logic in the composition of the board of directors of Southam Inc., for example, whose products are directed at least as much if not more toward women, and most of whose employees are women, including some of the senior employees. Yet, Southam's 1987 annual report indicates that the seventeen member board has only one woman, and the background of that one appears to have no direct or indirect relationship to the industry. Considering the nature of business in which Southam is engaged, and the long history of involvement by women in such business, it is surprising that there was not one woman among the twenty officers of the company, none among the nine officers of the Southam Printing Company, none among the eight executive officers of Coles Book Stores, and none among the eight executive officers of Southam Communications.

This is not a company that produces widgets, with a labour force of mechanics, machinists, and blacksmiths. This is a company that publishes fifteen daily newspapers, a financial weekly, and a variety of community and specialized publications. As well, Southam is involved in book retailing through its 189 stores throughout the country and is involved in information and communication services, with substantial interests in broadcasting, television, and cable services. The difference between the production of widgets and the production of services in which Southam is engaged is in the nature of employees involved in the respective processes: widgets are produced largely by skilled men; services are produced largely by women. Yet these women who are characterized by the president of the company as "engines that drive the company"[5] remain forever engines, not drivers.

The same absence of logic is evident in the composition of the board of the Hudson's Bay Company. The cover of the 1984 annual report is adorned almost entirely by women, reflecting the extent to which the company's commercial activity depends on women. Yet none of its executive officers are women, and there is one woman on its board of fifteen. It is problematical whether an executive of a forest products company, an aluminum company, or an energy company can provide more relevant and more effective advice on the nature of activities in which the Bay is engaged than an intelligent homemaker who manages a household budget involving purchases of foodstuffs and other supplies, appliances, and clothing for the entire age spectrum of the family.

Boards of directors are presumed to be constituted of individuals whose experience will contribute to the efficient management of the organization. The implication of this is that the individuals involved have experience in some aspect of the activities in which the company is engaged. Consider the case of Bell Canada Enterprises: the company employs large numbers of women, and its products and services are used by large numbers of women. A significant part of its operation is such as to classify it as a public utility, which has important public relations implications. Yet, its board is constituted largely of men, and significantly, of men whose experience is only remotely related to the activities of the company – a management consultant, a retired merchandiser, a petroleum company executive, a steel company executive, an executive of a distillery, a retired brewery executive, an automotive parts distributor, a retired medical person, an executive of a paper company. Such board compositions approach the composition of the Canadian Senate, where the selection process for appointment is a reward for services rendered to someone, rather than for the potential they have for contributions to the decision-making process of the enterprise.

The virtual absence of women from boards of directors and from the executive suites is not limited to commercial enterprises. They have been virtually excluded from public enterprises to an equal degree: the National Energy Board has no women; the board of the Bank of Canada has one woman, and all the forty-seven "principal officers" of the Bank are men; all sixteen executive officers of Petro-Canada are men; the board of the Canadian Broadcasting Corporation has two women, and there are only four women among the forty senior officers of the corporation.

Qualifications for Executive Positions

In search of justification for the relative absence of women from high-level positions in management, science, and technology, reference is often made to their alleged inadequacy in scientific and technical knowledge. The acceptance of such an explanation shifts the burden from employers to educational institutions, which allegedly have failed to "encourage" women to enter programs in mathematics, science, and technology, and to the women themselves for failing to choose programs that are "appropriate" for employment.

Such explanations are nothing more than rationalizations for discriminatory practices. An examination of the educational qualifications of men in senior managerial positions will establish that few of them possess high-level scientific and technical knowledge. Furthermore, there is no evidence that senior management positions require specialized mathematical and scientific knowledge for the efficient and effective performance of management functions. The decisions involved in such positions are management decisions, not scientific and technical decisions. Furthermore, if mathematical and scientific knowledge were a critical criterion for promotions to managerial positions, then it would have been natural to expect that some of the women with mathematical and scientific knowledge would have been in such positions. Few are to be found.

The false impression created by this rationalization for discriminatory practices has led to the equally false conclusion that future employment in desirable work activities will depend on mathematical and scientific knowledge and computer literacy. It is a false conclusion because most work activities do not require mathematical and scientific knowledge, and the use of computers and computer-related instruments and processes does not require computer literacy, in the sense of knowing how computers work.[6] Indeed, the efficient use of computer systems will require less knowledge for their operation than the driving of an automobile.

The relative absence of women from the higher echelons of business, government, and institutions will persist as long as women continue to be discriminated against in the allocation of work functions at the lower levels of the hierarchical structure. The critical criterion for accession to high-level positions is work experience and close associations with decision-makers at the higher levels of the structure. Therefore, the nature of work responsibilities assigned to individuals over time, the breadth of work responsibilities undertaken, the committees on which individuals collaborate in their work, the people in the higher echelons to whom individuals report, and the degree of initiative individuals are allowed will all determine the progress up the hierarchical pyramid.

It is often said that advancement in the upper echelons of the executive hierarchy depends to a considerable degree on whom you know. This is confirmed in a recent study of 132 women executives in the United States, 41.6 per cent of whom expressed the view that for progress up the corporate ladder "it is whom you know that matters, not what you know."[7] This is a generalization, perhaps, in relation to the "what you know" qualification, since it is doubtful that inadequate or limited knowledge will not be a barrier; nevertheless, "whom you know" becomes increasingly important in the highly competitive environment of the progressively narrowing pyramid as one ascends toward the top.

The extent to which experience has been an important variable is manifested in the virtual absence of women from high-level executive positions in enterprises and organizations that cater predominantly to women. Even some organizations in which women predominate as members have had disproportionate numbers of men in senior executive positions. For example, although the majority of members of public service unions are women, most paid union officers are men. In the United States, women make up 28.1 per cent of the membership of unions and employee associations, yet they hold none of the top executive positions and only a minority of the positions in the executive boards of their organizations.[8] The most likely reality in the United States, and in Canada, too, has been for women to have staff representation in the handling of grievances, in organizing employees, and in the conduct of educational programs in unions with relatively large proportions of women members. Also, they will be found in rank-and-file leadership positions in unions constituted predominantly of women, but not among the paid union officers, particularly paid officers off the shop floor.

Even in Sweden, which is commonly associated with equality in employment between men and women, occupational segregation is widespread. There, the Act on Equality Between Men and Women in Working Life, in effect since July 1, 1980, prohibits discrimination on the basis of sex in hiring, promotions, and training, yet there are very few women in the higher echelons of business and government, and, most surprising, women are almost nonexistent in the hierarchy of the champions of equality between the sexes, the trade union organizations. In 1982 almost 38 per cent of the membership of the Swedish Confederation of Trade Unions and 47 per cent of the membership of the Central Organization of Salaried Employees were women, yet their governing councils, executives, and senior officers were predominantly men.[9]

The foregoing suggests that the qualities that propelled women in increasing numbers to middle management positions in Canada over the past 10-15 years, such as appropriate professional and technical education, initiative, ambition, hard work, will not be sufficient for progress beyond middle management and into the executive suite. The qualities for entry into the executive suite are less structured and less formal than the qualities required for entry into lower-level employments and for rise to middle management positions. Breadth of work experience, exposure to decision-making under varying conditions and circumstances, and work with senior executives appear to be critical qualifications.[10] Women have had limited opportunities to acquire such qualifications, which explains the virtual absence of women from the executive suite. Consider, for example, the "Executive and Senior Management" group at Canada Trust (CT Financial Services Inc.), which in 1987 numbered 115. Canada Trust is a financial institution that has employed large numbers of women, over long periods of time, many with high-level academic qualifications. Yet there are only *three* women among the 115 executive and senior management officers.[11] The question arises, how many superior women were passed over by inferior men in the development of talents for executive and senior management responsibilities? Surely it cannot be argued that there were no women with appropriate educational qualifications and suitable employment characteristics for allocation to the executive stream.

The situation at Canada Trust is not an exception, of course. The same male dominance of the executive suite will be found in all major enterprises, whether commercial, industrial, or institutional. The few women chief executive officers of large ($50 million plus in sales) corporations in Canada are said to have inherited their positions from husbands or fathers.[12]

Progress with the integration of women into high-level jobs heretofore held by men will be slow. The positions in the organizational structure where work experience relevant for promotions to the executive suite is gained are occupied largely by men, and the required work experience is unstructured and undefined. When a requirement is undefined and unstructured it is open to variations to accommodate the experiences of those favoured for elevation. This puts the incumbents in a position of advantage that cannot be easily challenged. Progress with integration must begin with the reduction in discretionary powers, which as a first step requires some indication of the nature and extent of experience that is expected of candidates for elevation to senior executive positions.

Another condition that makes for slow progress is the slow rate of economic growth. Integration is easiest in periods of expansion and most difficult in periods of stability, stagnation, and decline. When a firm expands, new executive positions are created throughout the organizational structure. It is easier to fill such positions with women, since that does not entail the replacement of men, notwithstanding the implicit effect on men who aspire to the emerging positions. When firms decline or stagnate, quests for integration involve replacement of men by women. It is difficult to achieve any notable progress under such conditions.[13]

Women Executives in Government

The federal government is the largest single employer in the country. The three levels of government – federal, provincial, and municipal – and public institutions, such as schools, colleges, universities, and other educational and research institutes, hospitals, boards and commissions of all sorts, provide employment to more than one-third of the working population. Therefore, the public sector and public-sector-related employments can be an important catalyst in the process of change in the employment status of women in Canada. If governments were to take appropriate measures to reduce and ultimately eradicate differences in hiring and in the assignment of work responsibilities to men and women, and thereby cause the dispersion of women throughout the occupational and employment structures, competitive pressures will cause the private sector to respond accordingly. Had the proportion of the labour force employed by the public sector been smaller, the private sector could well ignore the terms and conditions of employment prevailing in it, or explain the different terms and conditions of employment on the basis of nebulous arguments used in the past, such as the different nature of work, different degrees of work intensity, security of employment, and so on. But, when public-sector employment is as large as it is now, fortuitous explanations will not do. Competition in the marketplace will dictate accommodation. The private sector will have to introduce the methods and processes of the public sector or risk the possibility of access to only second-rate employees.

A development of recent decades that increases the catalytic role of the public sector is the increase in the level, range, and quality of work performed in the public sector and in public-sector institutions. The activities of government have expanded so much and the significance of government in society and the economy has become so great as to make it necessary for government to employ large proportions of the most highly qualified men and women in the country. It can no longer be said that the best are in the private sector, the public sector taking the leftovers, the rejects of the private sector. The two labour markets that existed in the past, with limited competition between them, are no longer identifiable. Now the public and private sectors compete for the same men and women, which means that whatever incentives in terms and conditions of employment the one introduces the other must emulate.

Therefore, the ball of equality in employment opportunities and work responsibilities is fully in the court of the public sector. Its introduction there will make its introduction in the private sector a responsive dictate of the market.

The public sector has two characteristics that make for effective introduction of equality measures: one is the centralization of employment administration and regulation, including the administration of all terms and conditions of employment; the other characteristic is the budgetary control exercised by governments over public-sector institutions, which makes for effective enforcement of government regulations.

The record of senior management positions in the federal bureaucracy of Canada provides little encouragement for the advancement of women in the private sector. Although there is evidence of increasing participation by women in activities at the middle levels of the decision-making process, which gives the impression of change from their long-standing predominance in secretarial and clerical activities, they seem to remain at the middle management levels. As one moves higher and higher up the administrative hierarchy, women become fewer and fewer. The 1986 annual report of the Public Service Commission indicates that of the 4,351 executive (EX) and senior management (SM) positions, women held only 397: two out of 83 in the EX-5 category; 13 out of 214 in the EX-4 category; 27 out of 460 in the EX-3; 52 out of 745 in EX-2; and 93 out of 947 in EX-1. The remainder (210) were in the Senior Management category, out of a total of 1,902.

Table 3.2 contains information on men and women in executive and senior management positions in selected federal departments. Evidently, the federal government has not set a standard of employment equity worthy of emulation. Only the Privy Council Office has approached a level of representation of women in senior positions that may be considered respectable. The old boys' networks rule all other departments. Particularly lamentable are the efforts at External Affairs, where only 4.4 per cent of the positions are held by women, at Finance (7.6 per cent), Employment and Immigration (8.5 per cent), National Revenue (4.3 per cent), Transport (4.3 per cent), and Environment (6.3 per cent).

As indicated above, this relative absence of women from the senior ranks in industry, institutions, and the public service is not characteristic of Canada only. It is common to all countries, regardless of the level of their economic development and the nature of their political systems.

Does the evidence manifest discriminatory practices? Apologists

Table 3.2
**Women in Executive and Senior Management Positions in the
Federal Government, 1986 (selected departments)**

Department	Total No. of Positions	No. Held by Men	Per Cent	No. Held by Women	Per Cent
Treasury Board	65	57	87.7	8	12.3
Public Service Commission	69	53	76.8	16	23.2
Privy Council Office	77	48	62.3	29	37.7
Secretary of State	59	44	74.6	15	25.4
Employment and Immigration	200	183	91.5	17	8.5
External Affairs	455	435	95.6	20	4.4
Finance	92	85	92.4	7	7.6
Health and Welfare	143	122	85.3	21	14.7
National Revenue (Tax)	141	135	95.7	6	4.3
Transport	255	244	95.7	11	4.3
Consumer and Corporate Affairs	75	65	86.7	10	13.3
CIDA	113	101	89.4	12	10.6
Environment	238	223	93.7	15	6.4
All departments and agencies	4,351	3,954	90.9	397	9.1

SOURCE: Public Service Commission of Canada, *Annual Report 1986.*

insist it does not. It is alleged that men and women are given equal opportunity to demonstrate initiative, high-level skills, and leadership, and to sustain these qualities over time. It is argued that while women do demonstrate such qualities early in their working lives, many of them fail to sustain these qualities over time. Responsibilities associated with being a wife, homemaker, and mother allegedly tend to interfere with the continuous commitments expected of leaders. This is a rebuttable assertion. If the responsibilities associated with being homebound were a valid explanation for the failure of women to advance up the managerial and administrative hierarchy, then one would expect to find in senior management positions large numbers of women who do not have husbands and women who do not have children. There is no such evidence.

What, then, can explain this relative absence of women from leading positions in government, labour organizations, institutions, and industry in all countries, regardless of economic, social, and political structures? Do women have different personal and social values? Are women perhaps less ruthless than men in their relationships with actual and potential competitors? Do they respond to threat more protectively and less aggressively than men? These and many other such questions address the issue of personality characteristics, which may explain the significant differences in the distribution of women and men among occupations, between related occupations, and within occupations.

Responses to Occupational Segregation

The division of many occupations and employments into "male" and "female" is a common phenomenon in all countries, regardless of political systems, levels of economic development, and social structures. Some occupations are constituted largely of men and some largely of women: industrial workers and workers in skilled trades are predominantly men; clerical, service, and secretarial workers are predominantly women.

The question that has always generated discussion and controversy is the extent to which the segregation of jobs and the resulting characterization of employments as "male" and "female" manifest free choices, as opposed to the extent to which they manifest the existence of implicit and explicit discriminatory variables. Evidence of one or the other does not, of course, end the controversy, since the two are often interrelated and interactive: free choice is not really free if it is made in a social environment in which tradition dictates the employments that are "appropriate" for women, or in an employment environment where jobs are gender-labelled, or in a training and working environment designed for men or for women only. Men "chose" not to enter schools of nursing because nursing was not deemed appropriate for men, and the training and working environment, both within institutions and in the community at large, had female orientations. Women have faced similar barriers in the choices of engineering, dentistry, and business administration.

Segregation of men and women into different occupations not based on performance is a significant source of inefficiency in the allocation and use of human resources. It results in men and women entering employments in which their potential is underutilized. When a woman has demonstrated the ability to become a dentist and ends up becoming a dental hygienist instead, the stage is set for a number of inefficiencies: one is related to the failure to develop the full potential of a scarce human resource; a second arises from the possibility that a lesser potential was developed instead; yet a third arises from the fact that the two occupations are complementary to one another in the workplace. The feeling of injustice associated with being forced to choose the inferior alternative in training and employment, and the belief that if it were not for discriminatory barriers the complementary relationship may well be reversed, must necessarily impact on the working relationship and on the efficiency of the working processes. This applies equally to discriminatory practices and working relationships between doctors and nurses and among secretaries, administrative assistants, and different levels of management and administration.

Choice and Crowding in Occupations

The dominance of certain desirable occupations by men and the crowding of women in less desirable employments are commonly attributed to entry barriers: women have been barred from educational and training programs leading to the most desirable occupations, and selection and evaluation systems within institutional and commercial enterprises have been biased in favour of men. Yet, both the dominance and the crowding may well reveal different preferences. The argument that barriers are responsible is based on the assumption that men and women will not choose the same occupations if given free choice.

To the extent that dominance and crowding in occupations reflect free choices, the terms and conditions of employment that prevail in these must be deemed equitable. It must be assumed that some of the employment characteristics and conditions that are deemed negative are offset by terms and conditions with positive elements. In the absence of such offsetting elements, fewer people will choose those occupations, which will compel improvements in terms and conditions of employment.

Consider, for example, a situation in which men and women were given free choices to become physicians and, upon certification, to enter the employment of their choice. Without doubt, the specific employments into which physicians enter will become "crowded," which will depress their wages and cause relative deterioration in the working conditions. Would such an outcome be negative to society and to those who choose to become physicians? From society's standpoint the outcome will be favourable since it will likely result in a more efficient allocation of human resources than under conditions characterized by entry barriers to educational and training programs and obstacles in the choice of employment. From the standpoint of the individuals the outcome will also be favourable, since more individuals with potential will have the opportunity to become physicians, which may be more important to many of them than the earning of a relatively high income. Under such market conditions, those who, in their choices, are motivated by the potential monetary returns will choose other occupations. This example suggests that the outcomes of crowding are not necessarily negative to society and to individuals entering "crowded" occupations. Whether the outcomes are positive or negative depends not on the crowding itself but rather on whether the crowding is the result of free choices or the result of discriminatory practices.

Mandating Change and Fostering Change

There are two alternative approaches to the problem of employment discrimination: one is to mandate equality and compel managerial action; the other is to foster changes in consumer expectations and preferences. Laws mandating equality and directives compelling managerial action that are counter to demonstrated consumer preferences will not bring about the desired outcomes unless efforts are made at the same time to change consumer expectations. If consumers generally have greater confidence in men lawyers, equality in admissions into law programs, in admissions to the bar, and in employment will not bring equality to women lawyers. They will continue to be and feel disadvantaged. The objective should be to cause recognition by the population at large that differential outcomes in quality of work and efficiency are the result of preparation, ability, and experience, not the result of sex, age, nationality, and race.

Attitudes are very slow to change, of course, and the most effective means to attitude change is by demonstration. But this is conditional on being given the opportunity, which suggests a need for some form of directive to compel equal opportunity to entry into occupations, to employment, and to the assignment of employment responsibilities upon entry into employment. In short, women must be given an opportunity to demonstrate their capacities in the full range of occupations and in the full range of work functions associated with individual occupations. In the absence of such opportunity, employers will abide by the perceived preferences of consumers and preconceived notions of "appropriate" work functions for women and thereby continue to relegate women to secondary and ancillary employment positions.

In this context, the Employment Equity Act (1986) and the Federal Contractors' Program (1986) are meritorious approaches to the problem of occupational segregation. Even though limited in scope to enterprises with 100 employees or more, which in the context of the Canadian enterprise structure excludes most enterprises, these initiatives are a laudatory first step. Their effectiveness in giving women opportunities to demonstrate their capacities will depend, of course, on enforcement. The onus is now on the Canadian Human Rights Commission.

Historically, the segregation of women into inferior jobs had the effect of keeping out of the market all women who had a choice to work or not to work. Respectable women did not work outside family and home, and respectable men did not allow the women of the family to work away from home. The nature of most employments in which women engaged was such as to convey the impression that they worked for the money, which was interpreted to mean that they were not able to find themselves husbands or that they had husbands and fathers who failed to provide them adequate means of subsistence.[14] The stigma, for working women and their families, was in the nature of the work, not in the work itself. There was no stigma in socially acceptable work, but such work was generally limited.

Notes

1. Nancy S. Barrett, "Obstacles to Economic Parity for Women," *American Economic Review: Papers and Proceedings*, 72, 2 (May, 1982), pp. 160-65.
2. Two of these are discussed by Gail Warshofsky Lapidus in "Occupational Segregation and Public Policy: A Comparative Analysis of American and Soviet Patterns," in Martha Blaxall and Barbara Reagan, eds., *Women and the Workplace* (Chicago: University of Chicago Press, 1976), pp. 119-36.
3. This issue is examined by Janice F. Madden in "Comment III," *ibid*, pp. 245-50. Also see Francine D. Blau and Carol L. Jusenius, "Economists' Approaches to Sex Segregation in the Labour

Market: An Appraisal," *ibid*, pp. 181-99.

4. John G. Nicholson, "Equality on the Job Still Elusive Goal for Career Women in the Soviet Union," *The Globe and Mail*, December 12, 1986, p. A7. See also Lapidus, "Occupational Segregation."

5. Attributed to John P. Fisher, president of Southam Inc., *1987 Annual Report*.

6. T.S. Allen, *Computer World Canada*, 2 (9): 7 (March 4, 1985).

7. Robin L. Bartless and Timothy I. Miller, "Executive Compensation: Female Executives and Networking," *American Economic Review: Papers and Proceedings*, 75, 2 (May, 1985), pp. 266-70.

8. Barbara Mayer Wertheimer, "Women in the Labor Force," *Dialogue*, 2 (1985), p. 33.

9. Helen Ginsburg, *Full Employment and Public Policy in the United States and Sweden* (Lexington, Mass.: Lexington Books, 1983), p. 167.

10. Jac-André Boulet has asserted that improvements in the employment status of women are conditional on "changes in the educational system, skill development leave, and adult education." Such changes are effective for entry by women into more occupations, but are not the changes that will result in advancement by women to high executive positions. See "Occupational Diversification of Women in the Workplace," Economic Council of Canada, *Towards Equity* (Ottawa: Supply and Services Canada, 1985), pp. 31-41.

11. Canada Trust (CT Financial Services, Inc.), *Annual Report*, 1987.

12. Margaret Wente, "The Woman Who Never Was," *Canadian Business* (June, 1985), p. 259.

13. Kay Deaux and Joseph C. Ullman, *Women of Steel: Female Blue-Collar Workers in the Basic Steel Industry* (New York: Praeger, 1983).

14. Julie A. Matthaei, "Consequences of the Rise of the Two-Earner Family: The Breakdown of the Sexual Division of Labour," *American Economic Review: Papers and Proceedings*, 70 (May, 1980), pp. 198-202.

4

Computer Effects on Employment and Occupations

Introduction

Computers and computer-based instruments, processes, and products have been in existence for more than thirty years. They have revolutionized work in every area of activity: in farming, mining, and forestry; in manufacturing, construction, and transportation; in banking, insurance, and services; and even at home, at play, and in recreation. Physicians, nurses, and other health workers use them; engineers, architects, and accountants can no longer function without them; airline, railway, and water transportation would be paralysed without them; firefighters, the police, and the army cannot function without them; the operations of banks, trust companies, the stock markets, and other financial institutions would come to a standstill without them; and so will all communications systems, many offices, and most laboratories.

Yet this revolution in work and work organization has been achieved almost imperceptibly. Somehow, the old ways of doing things were set aside and new ways were put into effect without any significant opposition, and in most instances without any major difficulties. Even executives, who associated the keyboard with their female secretaries, have accepted the technology and have become personally involved with it.

The explanation for the relatively imperceptible accommodation of computer technology is not difficult to find: it has made work easier and faster; it has not had any serious adverse employment effects on large numbers of people; and it did not require very much effort for people to become proficient in its use. Had large numbers of people been affected adversely and had it required high-level training, with associated risks of failure, the conversion of processes to the computer would have become much more visible.

The characteristics of the technology[1] provide an explanation for its rapid introduction. (1) It can collect, monitor, detect, and recognize information, which means it has *the capacity to capture information.* (2) It can convert information to digital form and retain it in memory to be retrieved whenever required, which is *a capacity to store information.* (3) It can arrange and re-arrange information, perform calculations, and produce configurations, which is *a capacity to manipulate information.* (4) It can transmit, display, and move information electronically, which is *a capacity to distribute information.* (5) It can provide information feedback on operations, which facilitates operational control of equipment, production processes, output, and quality, which is *a capacity to control entire ranges of production activities.*

Employment Implications

Contrary to generally held notions that computers and computer-related instruments, processes, and products are substitutes for labour, many are in fact complementary to labour and substitutes for capital. For example, the word processor substituted the typewriter and complemented the typist, increasing the typist's (word processor operator's) productivity. Whatever substitution of typists may take place will be via the increase in productivity, which will depend on the relationship between the increase in the volume of output and the increase in productivity.

The employment implications to date have been generally positive: on the production side, a large number of new employments have been created in the production, distribution, sales, and maintenance of the new technologies; on the operation side, the occupations of programmers and analysts have become established in the occupational structure; and a number of existing occupations have become reclassified to reflect their new work functions – from "clerical" to "data control," from "clerk-typist" to "data entry," from "office equipment operators" to "computer operators," and so on.

It is significant that all such occupational reclassifications have involved limited retraining. The widespread notion that employment in computerized processes is conditional on the possession of high-level technical and scientific knowledge does not find support in the occupational mixes of such processes. The jobs that require such knowledge are relatively few in number. The work functions of the vast majority are non-technical, notwithstanding the job titles assigned to them.

For example, how much technical and scientific knowledge does one need to operate a computer? Considering that children are becoming proficient operators, despite their limited education and work experience, suggests very little scientific and technical knowledge is required. Similarly, how much knowledge of computers and telecommunications technology does a bank teller need to perform efficiently the work functions involved in the job, such as accessing the computer, depositing information in it, and requesting information from it? Not very much.

Indeed, a comparative assessment of knowledge and other employment characteristics needed for the teller's job before and after computerization, which involved the manual recording of credits and debits into personal bankbooks, rapid mental calculations of balances, and the maintenance of up-to-date credit and debit card accounts, needed more knowledge and a higher level of mental activity than do computerized work functions. This is a common experience with the computerization of existing work functions, which suggests varying degrees of deskilling in traditional occupations.

A related development, with significant implications for the employment of women, is the change in the functional characteristics of some jobs, which has made them accessible to men and women alike. The categorization and typecasting of jobs as primarily women's and primarily men's had the effect of limiting competition for them. The possibility now exists of computers and computer-related instruments eroding some of the discriminatory characteristics and making jobs more unisexual, which will increase competition for them. It had become traditional, for example, to associate women with the keyboard of a typewriter, and when word processors made their appearance it was quite natural to think of women as their operators. The advent of the personal computer, with word-processor capabilities and attached printers, has introduced men to the keyboard. To the extent that technology reduces the physical characteristics of work activities that typecast them as men's activities and women's activities, greater efficiency should be expected in the allocation of human resources. If men and women alike are able to move freely into those activities that offer the highest rewards, optimal allocative efficiency will be achieved and sustained.

The increasing appearance of men at the keyboards of computers is eroding the dominance of women in keyboard-related work. Therefore, the replacement of the typewriter, the filing, the charting, and other office work activities with the computer and computer-related instruments can be expected to increase competition from men for some of the jobs traditionally performed by women. On the other hand, there is increasing evidence that employment is shifting from manufacturing and some services to information activities.[2] This tends to favour women. Over time, we have witnessed shifts from primary-sector work (agriculture, mining, forestry, fishing, and hunting) to secondary-sector work (manufacturing, construction, transportation), and then to tertiary-sector work (government services, health and education services, personnel and business services). These shifts in employment and the accompanying changes in the work activities were positive to the employment of women, evidenced by the significant increase in the employment of women over the past three decades. The creation of work now in the fourth sector – the information sector – gives promise that the work lost in the tertiary (service) sector will be more than made up, just as the work created in the service sector over the past three decades more than made up for the work lost in agriculture and manufacturing.

An important characteristic of the work performed in the information sector is that it is *gender neutral*. In other words, unlike the work of programmers and analysts, which has come to be associated with men, most information work has no association with either men or women. This will increase employment opportunities for women. Indeed, despite the connotations of "programmer" and "analyst" as male jobs, the expanding field of "software" production remains relatively open.

The International Standards Organization defines "software" as "intellectual creation comprising the programmes, procedures, rules and any associated documentation pertaining to the operation of a data processing system. Software is independent of its carrier media." Software is the brain of the computer and information technology infrastructure: computers, word processors, terminals, telecommunications systems, automated systems in industry and transportation, in offices, in distribution, data banks, electronic funds transfer systems, automated industrial and consumer instruments and products, defence systems, and so on all function through software. The functions the systems perform and their efficiency and effectiveness depend on the quality of the software.[3] Considering the high complexity of the multitude of activities performed in the economy and society at large by governments, institutions, and enterprises, the production and distribution of software will eventually emerge as a most significant area of human activity. To date, this has been one of the activities that has experienced manpower shortages. The main reason for this has been the relatively limited period since the introduction of the new technology. It takes time to build a stock of appropriately educated and trained people in a new field of endeavour.

If women were to adopt an aggressive approach in competition for jobs in the expanding information sector, men will increasingly find themselves at a competitive disadvantage: stripped of the advantage of gender association, which has favoured them in almost all desirable employments, men will enter the market as equals with women.

All that one would need to do then is to change the attitudes of women about the nature of employments for which to prepare themselves. Given appropriate preparation, men and women can share equally in the emerging employment opportunities. Evidence from England, however, indicates that career choices made by women continue to reflect traditional stereotyping. A survey of school leavers found that girls fantasized about becoming airline stewardesses, nursery nurses, kennel maidens, pop singers, fashion models, and top secretaries, while the boys produced a list of about 100 occupations, including spaceman, millionaire, veterinarian, football player, artist, and politician. None of the girls indicated any desire for factory work of any kind, and none indicated interest in apprenticeship programs, except hairdressing. The boys, on the other hand, expressed keen interest in apprenticeships.[4]

The Overall Employment Effect

The positive employment effects to date do not mean, of course, that they will continue to be positive in future, as the technology evolves from the present still largely stand-alone units and stations to fully integrated and interactive computer telecommunications systems and networks. The extent of interface between the technology and human labour in such a system and the nature of the interface remain uncertain. In light of this uncertainty, we can only speculate by reference to three approaches.

The first is the reality that we do not really know what will happen to individual occupations because we do not know precisely the nature of instruments, processes, and products that will ultimately evolve out of this experimental period, nor do we know the nature of work activities that will emerge. Looking back in time, stenographers and telephone operators comprised major occupations thirty years ago, providing employment to thousands; clerks were largely men 100 years ago; typists hardly existed fifty years ago; and key-punch operators emerged as a significant computer-related occupation twenty years ago, only to disappear within ten years. Some of the computer-related occupations now in employment may disappear as well within the next decade or two.

The second is the certainty that knowledge on the entire broad range of science, technology, economy, and society will continue to expand, and the expansion in knowledge dictates the creation of specializations in smaller and smaller increments of knowledge. That translates into additional occupations and occupational categories.

The third is that invisible process which converts increasing productivity and decreasing unit costs and prices into incomes, demand, and employment. The technology that increases productivity and reduces employment also reduces the cost per unit of output, which in turn becomes reflected in lower unit prices, higher incomes, or both. Whether the result is lower prices or higher incomes, it will lead to an increase in demand for goods and services generally, which will result in more employment. With higher incomes people tend to travel more, purchase more entertainment, eat out more, and purchase more recreational, personal, and household services. All these involve significant employment.

Many of the work activities that seem to disappear with the introduction of new technology do not in fact disappear; rather, the technology causes changes in the structure and organization of work, which then dictates the reorganization, redefinition, and relocation of the work activities. Consider, for example, the occupation of domestic servant to which reference is made above: it has virtually disappeared. But the work continues to be done, except it is now being done by employees of commercial enterprises – maid services, rug cleaners, furniture polishers, window cleaners, etc. It appears that the decrease in supply of women willing to tie themselves to specific households in master-servant relationships, the increasing participation of women in full-time paid work and the associated need for occasional help with household work activities, the convenience for households in having a bonded commercial enterprise perform maintenance services for brief periods once every week or two instead of a permanent servant in the family, and such other considerations dictated accommodative changes in the structure and organization of domestic work.

Similar restructuring may well take place with the introduction of integrated computer and telecommunications systems, which are expected to facilitate the execution of many work activities from wherever the individual has access to the required computer and the required information. Such a system will induce dispersion in employment, in contrast to the concentration in employment that has been the trend since the industrial revolution. Dispersion may well be manifested in increasing numbers of independent "consultants" who will do work now performed within organizations by research assistants, programmers, and analysts, word-processor operators who also perform proofing and editing functions, financial, marketing, and communications experts. What happens in effect is that the occupational classifications change, the organization of the work changes, but the work functions remain largely the same. Independent practitioners become employees; employees become independent practitioners; office clerks become data control clerks; office machine operators become computer operators; typists become data entry operators, VDT operators, and word-processor operators; and so on. When the employment effects of technological changes are examined from such a perspective, the conclusions are not as gloomy as they appear when the focus is on employment affected negatively.

Furthermore, the technology that is changing the structure of occupations and employment is not limited to computer technology. Biotechnology, fibre optics, and laser technology are having significant positive employment effects. They will provide the capital instruments and processes needed for the revitalization of stagnating and declining industries, increase the efficiency of individuals and processes, create new instruments, processes, and products, and provide the basis for diversification in the mix of economic activity. Biotechnology alone is expected to bring about very significant changes in the economic infrastructure, in nutrition, in health, in energy.[5] The employment implications of these new technologies for research and development and in products, methods of production, and distribution are vast.

Changes in the Organization of Work

The potential effects of computer technologies on the employment of women are related, of course, to the activities in which women engage. Three groups of activities can be identified: those which relate to home and family; those which relate to employment for pay; and all other activities, including volunteer work and leisure. Involvement in the three is interrelated: for example, the increase in the participation of women in work activities for pay in the past three decades is attributed in part to the increasing use of technologies in household activities; similarly, the increasing use of technologies in employment activities and the subsequent increase in productivity made it possible to reduce hours of work per day, week, year, and increase the time available for volunteer work and leisure.

Household Activities and the Household Economy

Household and family-related activities have played a pivotal role in the allocation of time by women to market activities: tradition has dictated that women bear primary responsibility for home and family, and tradition has prevailed despite the significant changes over time in the nature of work and the amount of work involved. Washing machines, dryers, and synthetic fibres have changed significantly laundering and ironing activities; vacuum instruments and cleaning fluids have changed the housecleaning functions; electrical and mechanical kitchen instruments and factory-prepared mixes and foods have changed the preparation of meals; and television has changed significantly the activities that relate to family education and recreation. All of these have changed the organization of household activities, the allocation of time to each range of activities, and the effort involved in them. Yet, they have remained largely the responsibility of one person – the woman, the wife, the mother. If women have some special characteristics, aptitudes, and training for such activities, efficiency considerations would have dictated such an outcome. But they have limited training in the managerial and functional household responsibilities they are expected to assume.[6] Limited training and the inefficiencies associated with it have provided the impetus for capital investment in household activities, which will probably continue as long as the responsibility remains largely in the hands of relatively untrained members of the household, who would rather do something else.

This suggests that the household economy will become increasingly more capital-intensive, particularly with the advent of microelectronic instruments and processes appropriate for household activities. Indeed, Jonathan Gershuny expects a progressive expansion in the productive capacity of households, as microelectronic and telecommunications processes make it possible to transfer increasing numbers of production activities from the commercial sector to the household sector.[7] The microwave and factory-prepared foodstuffs have reduced the labour involved in the preparation of meals and increased the efficiency of the process; the computer and telecommunications technologies will reduce the labour and increase the efficiency in activities related to planning, scheduling, budgeting, and generally managing the household; and modulated educational and recreational programs will reduce the labour and increase the quality of educational and recreational activities in the household. To the extent that the decrease in labour intensity of household activities has been a factor in the increase in participation rates of women, the further reductions in labour intensity can be expected to result in further increases in the labour force participation rates of women.

Integrating the Household Economy and the Market Economy

Considering that women continue to be primarily responsible for work associated with home and family, the potential effect of computer technology on the organization of work is of special interest. Speculation on the matter has focused on the possibility that the home and the place of work will be computer-linked, which will make it possible to integrate all forms of work activity. Although some women have interpreted such speculation as an attempt by men to avoid sharing in the work involved with home and family, the computer-link of home and office will facilitate as much work from home for men as for women. To the extent that men can do some of their office work from home, they will remain at home longer, which may well result in more sharing in work related to home and family than at present. The evolution of such a development may well evolve into the integrated system of work organization that existed before the onset of the factory system and the centralized commercial system.

Before the industrial revolution, the work roles of men and women were not as divergent as they evolved subsequently. Work and home were linked, and men, women, and children worked together at home-based activities in shops and on the land. The industrial revolution and the concentration of production in factories separated paid work from home and men from their families. Women remained at home, while men went to work. This brought about three lasting effects on women and their families: men were separated from the routine of daily family life; women and children became economically dependent on men; and housework and child-care became separated from income-earning work.[8]

Over time, the evolution of industrial economies into commercial and service economies created work deemed appropriate for women, which resulted in increasing participation by women in work activities outside the home, but the divergent roles of men and women remained in both paid work and household work. Even though women entered into paid employment, it was regarded as secondary to the work men did, and they remained primarily responsible for the work related to home and family.

The question now arises whether the advent of the information revolution will reverse the process of divergence and bring about a convergence again in the respective roles. The personal computer and telecommunications technologies seem to be making it possible for men and women to work at home; consequently, the work of the formal market economy and the work of the informal household economy seem to be converging in the manner of work prior to the industrial revolution.

The possibility of earning an income at home has been a reality for increasing numbers of people over the years, as the work of more and more people changed from that which could only be performed in the place of employment – the assembly line, the forest, the shop, the office – to work that could be done any time at any place. The typist and the teacher could take work home; the salesperson working in such fields as insurance and real estate could arrange the schedule so as to do more of the work from home; so could the planner, the engineer, the accountant, and so on. The issue has not been the ability to work away from the place of work, but rather commitment to the work, organization of the work, and the degree of satisfaction derived from the work. The computer and telecommunications technologies will facilitate work continuity and the dispersion of work; whether people will turn that technological facility into opportunity to work from home, and to use the system on a continuous basis, will depend on the extent to which they derive satisfaction from the activity.

Nevertheless, the integration of computers and telecommunications systems into interactive networks does promise the evolution of a form of work organization that provides for greater flexibility than that in existence at present in most work settings. The computer will provide the work-related information, respond to work-related questions, and accept, reproduce, and communicate memoranda, reports, letters, and any other information at any time. Considering that the computer's location is of no consequence to the performance of the work tasks, those who have access to it, work with it, and work through it with others can themselves be at any location. As long as all are linked together to the computer and have access to it, they can be at home or the world over, travelling by car or plane, anywhere. The implications of this for work processes, the organization of work, people-work interfaces, work at home, interpersonal relationships, indeed, for society at large, are immense.

The most likely development that will link work at the workplace and work at home is the increase in levels of education and the increasing professionalization of work. In professional work it is difficult to separate work activities and non-work activities. Even leisure becomes largely work, in the sense that the work is largely mental activity, which goes on all the time. Therefore, the level of work will determine the degree of involvement in its performance, not the technology with which the work is performed. The technology will facilitate continuity; whether continuity will become a pattern in work activity will depend on the nature of changes that work itself will undergo. The possibility of gradual confluence between work and leisure will dissipate the distinction between the two, thereby bringing about a significant change in society at large: there would no longer be such things as work, workplace, work time, away from work, holiday, etc. The distinction between work and non-work may well disappear.

Employment in the Market Economy

The potential decrease in demand for labour in the household economy raises the question of the capacity of the market economy to provide employment to increasing numbers of women who will be seeking employment. The critical question is, then: what will happen to employment in parts of the market economy that recorded increasing rates of employment over the past three or four decades, namely, trade, finance, insurance, real estate, and services? The majority of working women are employed in these industry groups. Let us look at each industry group.

Retail and wholesale work employs close to one million women, mainly in retail activities. The introduction of technology is not likely to impact significantly on this kind of employment, notwithstanding the trend to self-service. There is no indication of any alternative forms of service in the thousands of specialty retail stores selling clothes, shoes, jewellery, confectioneries, and the like. The pending introduction of point-of-sale systems (POS) and their integration to electronic funds transfer systems (EFTS) will affect adversely the employment of some cashiers, inventory control clerks, and accounts clerks, but the numbers adversely affected are expected to be relatively small. On balance, then, knowledgeable persons in the industry expect existing trends to continue, which in recent years have shown modest increases in employment.

The finance, insurance, and real estate industries employ close to 400,000 women, mainly in secretarial, clerical, typing, and sales activities. Electronic technology, in the form of information processing, text processing, nation-wide on-line communications systems, integrated computer-communications transaction terminals, and automatic debiting and crediting of commercial transactions in deposit accounts is expected to impact severely on employment, particularly in finance and insurance. For example, with personal computer access to bank accounts, all production functions associated with banking activities will be performed by computers – deposits, transfers, payments, the keeping of records, etc. The introduction of EFTS, POS, and automatic teller machines will effectively transfer most of the activities currently performed in the widely dispersed branches of banks to the computers of bank customers. The finance industry will undergo increasing organizational concentration, and the activities now performed by branches of banks and trust companies will become widely dispersed, automatic, and invisible as work functions.

It should be expected that by the middle of the 1990s the organizational structure of finance, insurance, and real estate will change significantly. In particular, the automatic teller machines will become automatic financial services machines, which will dispense information and perform a wide variety of transactional functions ranging from the usual banking functions currently performed to the purchase of travellers' cheques and other instruments of exchange, the purchase of insurance, the sale and purchase of bonds and securities traded at stock exchanges, and so on. Furthermore, the integration of computers and telecommunications systems into networks will link together all institutions, commercial enterprises, and households, which will facilitate computer-initiated and computer-executed transactions.

On the other hand, in recent years financial institutions have demonstrated a high degree of aggressiveness in the provision of financial services. A wide range of new services has been introduced and marketed, which creates employment. This is the explanation for the continued expansion of employment in the finance, insurance, and real estate sector, notwithstanding the widespread introduction of computers and computer-related instruments.

The service industries employ close to 2.6 million women. These are very diverse industries with wide-ranging work activities. From the chambermaid to the Governor General, the labour force of the service sector contains almost all of the occupations employed in the goods-producing sector and many more. There are found in it workers with very low levels of education and very high levels; low skill, no skill, and very high skill; the very young delivering papers house to house and the very old commissionaire; the politician and the bureaucrat, the lobbyist and the gambler, the croupier and the bouncer, the day-care worker, the counsellor, the nurse, the artist, the researcher, the performer, the doctor, the lawyer, and thousands of other work classifications.

The wide range of services and the considerable heterogeneity of the people performing them mean that service jobs are less vulnerable to changes in technology than jobs involving a narrow range of activities. Standardized, narrowly defined, and specific jobs are more at risk than jobs that are wide ranging and varied. Even in areas of activity where the range of services appears concentrated, such as office work, services to business, and personal services, the nature and environment of the work involved is so diverse that it is difficult to generalize about the nature or extent of the impact on work and employment. The computer, the word processor, and the information bank can complement and speed up the work of the secretary, the lawyer, the writer, the teacher, the doctor, the nurse, the bus driver, the policeman, but will not reduce significantly the wide range and continuously changing work variables they encounter. Every work activity involving people rendering services to people is subject to continuous change; and the more changeable it is, the more unstructured its functions must be.

Women in Computer-Related Occupations

The effects of computer technology on the employment of women appear positive on balance: new occupations and employments have been created, many of which remain in short supply even after three decades of computer use. Even jobs that were expected to be severely reduced in numbers, such as secretarial, clerical, typing, and accounting and bookkeeping, have in fact increased in numbers. What happened in reality was a change in the performance of work functions: some typists are feeding the system with information, which now makes them "information entry operators"; some clerks file tapes, which makes them "tape librarians"; other clerks distribute the output of the system among interested parties, which makes them "information control clerks"; and there continue to be, of course, scheduling clerks, accounts clerks, and general filing clerks. Similarly, some secretaries have become "administrative assistants" and "special assistants," others have become "administrative officers," and still others have become "research assistants."

However, the record of employment in computer-related work indicates that women have once again allowed this comparatively new and potentially dominant field to become dominated by men and typecast as a field of work more appropriate for men than for women. The predominance of men in managerial and professional positions has created a conceptual association of "computers," "telecommunications," and "programmer-analysts" with men, while the predominance of women in "data entry," "data control," and "computer operation" has created a conceptual association of women with secondary support staff service positions. This is, of course, a continuation of the traditional distribution of men and women in the occupational structure, notwithstanding the fact that the traditional has been wasteful. The typecasting of occupations by sex has resulted in much misallocation and underutilization of valuable human resources. It is most important that typecasting be avoided in relation to emerging fields of employment.

The following two tables demonstrate the extent to which the tradition of old has crept into the new: men occupy almost all executive and management positions, almost all supervisory positions, and most professional positions, whereas women are relegated to the traditional support staff positions. In a relatively large computer services system of an academic institution (Table 4.1) all six executive level positions of directors and associate directors were occupied by men, and so were thirteen of fifteen assistant director positions; also, thirty-two of fifty programmer-analyst positions were occupied by men. Tradition has even crept into the few managerial and professional positions that were occupied by women: the two women assistant directors were responsible for activities commonly associated with women – support services and information services, respectively; and of the eighteen women programmer-analysts, only three occupied senior positions. On the computer operations side, men occupied all supervisory and senior operating positions, whereas women occupied most of the secretarial, clerical, and typing positions, some of which have been reclassified and renamed "data entry," "data control," "tape librarian," and "computer operator."

In addition to the computer services system, the academic institution has a computer science teaching and research department constituted of twenty-four academic staff, three technicians, nine research staff, one programmer-analyst, one systems architect, one project manager, and five secretaries. One woman is on the academic staff at the instructor level of the professorial hierarchy; the technicians and the research staff are all men, and so are the programmer-analyst and the systems architect. The project manager is a woman, and so are the five secretaries.

Affiliated with the academic institution is a Computer Modelling Group, which employs fifteen computer-related professionals and two secretaries. Two of the fifteen professionals are women, and so are the two secretaries. And there are also, of course, a significant num-

Table 4.1

Employment of Men and Women in a Major Computer System of a Public Institution, 1985

	Total	Men	Women
Executive level (2 directors, 4 associate directors)	6	6	0
Assistant directors and unit managers	15	13	2
Unit co-ordinators (technical specialists)	4	4	0
Programmer-analysts:			
Senior level	15	12	3
Working level	21	13	8
Entry level (university graduate)	12	6	6
Entry level (tech-school graduate)	2	1	1
Computer operations:			
Operations supervisor	1	1	0
Shift supervisors	3	3	0
Senior computer operator	1	1	0
Working-level computer operators	5	4	1
Computer operator trainees	3	2	1
Data entry supervisor	1	0	1
Data entry operators	5	0	5
Production analysts (data controllers)	3	2	1
Dispatch clerks	4	2	2
Administrative and secretarial:			
Administrative assistants to directors	2	0	2
Administrative secretaries	2	0	2
Tape librarian	1	0	1
Secretaries and clerk-typists	3	0	3
Accounts clerk	1	0	1
Bookstore clerk	1	0	1
Storekeeper	1	1	0
Total	112	71	41

ber of computer-related employments dispersed among individual departments throughout the institution – in engineering, medicine, the science departments, the library, the faculty of education, and so on – and in all of them the distribution is the same: almost all professional positions are occupied by men, and almost all support staff positions are occupied by women.

Table 4.2 contains the employment record of the information systems department of a large commercial enterprise. The distribution of positions between men and women is roughly the same as that of the computer systems in the public institution: all seven management positions were occupied by men, as well as forty of the fifty-six programmer-analyst positions. Women occupied only one of thirteen senior analyst positions and four of eleven senior programmer positions. But all seven tape librarians were women, and so were all thirteen data entry operators.

All information on computer-related employments indicates that a significant number of jobs have been created over the past two decades in systems management, programming, operations, design and production, demonstration and sales, and many other computer-related activities, yet women appear to have remained in ancillary positions.

New and expanding fields of employment usually present the greatest opportunities for entry and advancement: job typecasting is more limited in them than in established employments, and there are no traditions that ban or limit employment. Yet, women do not appear to have taken advantage of the opportunity and have allowed the general traditional allocations of employment between men and women to become established in this field as well: men in managerial, professional, and technical positions; women in secretarial, clerical, and other support positions. Undoubtedly, the early association of the technology with engineering and mathematics caused entry problems for women; nevertheless, there is no evidence of any substantial and sustained efforts by women with requisite qualifications to enter the field. More than twenty years passed before women began to register in university computer science programs.

The expectation that computer technology will reduce significantly the number of jobs at the bottom of the occupational hierarchy, which are largely occupied by women, and increase the number of jobs at the higher levels of the hierarchy, which are largely occupied by men, is yet to materialize. Experience to date indicates a structural change in employment, manifested in the shift of low-level jobs from the general office to the non-technical operational level of the computer system. There is evidence of an increase in the number of middle management positions but no evidence of an overall decrease in low-level positions or of any significant change in technical positions. What appears to have happened is a structural change involving the substitution of occupations within the same levels in the occupational structure: general office clerks with data control clerks; office typists with data entry operators; and a shift in employment from one area of activity (the general office) to another (the department of information

Table 4.2

Employment in an Information Systems Department of a Large Commercial Enterprise, 1981

	Total employment	Men	Women
Manager of data processing	1	1	0
Manager of computer resources	1	1	0
Manager – administration	1	1	0
Manager – systems analyst	1	1	0
Senior computer analysts	13	12	1
Junior computer analysts	7	4	3
Manager – programming	1	1	0
Senior programmers	11	7	4
Junior programmers	19	12	7
Manager – data base administration	1	1	0
Data base analysts	6	5	1
Manager – computer operations	1	1	0
Tape librarians	6	0	6
Data control clerks	4	3	1
Computer operators	13	8	5
Scheduling clerk	1	0	1
Data entry operators	13	0	13
System security specialist	1	1	0
Hardware planner	1	1	0
Secretaries	7	0	7
Totals			
Managerial	7	7	0
Professional	56	40	16
Other	46	13	33
Grand total	109	60	49

SOURCE: S. G. Peitchinis, *The Employment Implications of Computers and Telecommunications Technology*, Report #5412-4-5 (Ottawa: Department of Communications, 1981).

systems).

In summary, women appear to have been slow to take advantage of high-level employment opportunities associated with the management and operation of the new technologies. The employment positions they occupy in the new technological infrastructure are for the most part at the same levels in the occupational pyramid as they have occupied in the old infrastructure. It is as if women were given a choice between employment security and advancement, and they chose security. But there is evidence of change in this with the increasing entry of women in university programs in computer science, business administration, and engineering.

Technology, Productivity, and Employment

The historical record indicates that in the general relationship between technology and employment, the critical issue is whether productivity is increasing and the economy is expanding. When major technological changes were accompanied by rising productivity and economic growth, employment generally increased and employment dislocations were generally accommodated successfully in alternative employments; problems of unemployment only arose when productivity and economic growth remained at relatively low levels. Given economic growth, defined in terms of increases in the volume of marketable goods and services, employment can be created even if the increasing volume of marketable goods and services is produced largely by capital and natural resources, with only minimal participation by workers.

This suggests the existence of two kinds of employment: one, in conjunction with capital and natural resources, produces the national output, and the other is the result of the national output. One involves the production of the goods and services that enter into the gross national product, the other is the result of the distribution and expenditure of the national income. This proposition is in conflict with established economic theory, which regards all employment as contributing to the national output. Yet, we all know of work that depends largely or entirely on income distribution via governments and through philanthropy, and whose contributions to the national output of goods and services is difficult to measure. Consider, for example, the services of the family member assigned responsibility for home and family. The value of the services is not included in the national income even though these services are the same in nature as those provided in commercial laundries, bakeries, restaurants, nurseries and kindergartens, and many other areas of the income-producing economy.

The economic explanation for this problem is that the services rendered by members of the family to members of the family at home by-pass the marketplace and therefore do not enter into the pricing and exchange system. This means, of course, that if families were to give up providing services to themselves and allowed all services related to home and family to be provided by commercial establishments, employment would increase by millions. In the absence of economic growth such a development would result in massive income redistribution and a general decrease in living standards; but given that it would involve a massive redistribution in employment, it is conceivable that the national output would increase and more than offset the increase in job creation, which would increase living standards. Clearly, it all depends on the assumptions one makes about the relationship between employment and national income.

What is suggested here is that while most employment is functionally related to the national output, in the sense of contributing to that output, some employment is *the result* of the national output, in the sense of being created by the ability of the economy to pay. Applying this to the payment of wages and salaries and to the wage structure, it means that while the wages of most are presumed to reflect the relative contributions they make to the value of goods and services they produce, the wages paid to some reflect their relative positions in the employment structure. When examined from such a perspective, the wage structure will be found to perform two functions: an *allocative function*, in the allocation of human resources among employment activities that produce the goods and services entering into the calculation of the national output, and a *distributive function*, in its performance as a mechanism for the distribution of the national income.

The significance of the latter is yet to be examined with the intensity it warrants. Competitive economic theory ascribes to the wage structure both efficiency in the allocation of human resources and equity in the distribution of income. To the extent that there exists a functional relationship between employment and the production of the national output, and the payment of wages and salaries reflects the relative contributions of the wage and salary recipients to the value of goods and services, the proposition of efficiency and equity will be sustained. But to the extent that such is not the case, and some people receive less than their contributions to the value of output while others receive substantially more than their contributions, then the structure will be violating both efficiency and equity. But then, it is difficult to measure relative contributions to the value of output. Hundreds of people are involved in the production of an automobile, for example, from designers, testers, and assembly-line workers to secretaries, engineers, and managers. What contribution does each of them make to the value of automobile?

In view of this difficulty, the matter becomes one of perception and general social acceptance: as long as people at large believe that the wage and salary structure reflects the relative contributions of the various workers, it will remain a convenient and effective mechanism for the allocation of human resources among employment activities and for the distribution of income. And the uncertainty about relative contributions, particularly in public-sector employment, makes it possible to create employment at all levels of the wage and salary structure. When there is no market price for the service, as in the case of the public sector, and therefore cost-price relationships do not exist, employment creation is limited by cost only, which is the ability to pay. The ability of the public sector to pay depends on its revenue, which is generally related to the growth of the economy. Therefore, given economic growth, employment will be created, even though the production of an increasing range of goods and services may become increasingly capital-intensive.

Quest for Work and Distribution of Work

Concerns about the employment effects of computer technology are founded in part on the expectation that computers and computer-related instruments and processes will produce more of the total output of goods and services, and there will be less work for people who want to work.

People who want to work do so for two main reasons: to earn their means of subsistence, and for their physiological, psychological, and social well-being. There are many people who do not need to work for their subsistence, yet they work, and many of them work long and hard for their well-being and for the accumulation of wealth; and there are many people who seem quite able to maintain their social well-being without work, but they work for their subsistence. In our social and economic system most of the people work for both reasons.

If technology produces more and more of an increasing national output of goods and services, then the problem of subsistence will not be one of availability of goods and services for a rising standard of living for all but one of distribution of the goods and services. Given a system of distribution that meets some social criteria for equity, and economic criteria for efficiency in the allocation of resources to productive activities, the association of employment with income would be eroded further. Such erosion has been in effect for some time, of course, indicated by the incomes of people who receive pensions, unemployment insurance, disability insurance, welfare, and other forms of payment not related to participation in the production of the current output of goods and services. The possibility that technology will produce more goods and services means simply an increase in the capacity of the economy to make more payments to more people who do not participate in economic activity.

This raises the question of whether there are more people who would rather not participate in economic activity but who do so because of the link between income and employment – people who would prefer to retire earlier, people who would prefer to stay in school longer, people who would work fewer days and fewer hours per day, and people who would prefer a more discontinuous pattern of worklife than the one in effect at present, which dictates continuous participation over a lifetime of work. The answer is yes: even in the existing system of limited income guarantees, people are retiring earlier, staying in school longer, and returning to school after a number of years of employment. As well, part-time employment is increasing, and increasing numbers of people take time off work without pay for varying periods.

These trends should change our perception of the role of work in human activity. The notion that people need to work for physiological, psychological, and social reasons addresses the matter of the need for participation in activity for personal satisfaction and socialization, not for the sake of the work itself or for the income it provides. The concern has been that people would not be able to occupy themselves beneficially in the absence of assigned work. Yet, the evidence indicates a contrary development: each successive generation has been allocating less time to work for the purpose of earning an income and more time to other activities. Entry into employment has been progressively postponed by the majority of people by as much as eight to ten years over the past century – from age eight to ten, to age eighteen to twenty; exit from full-time employment has been progressively earlier, particularly over the past two decades; vacation periods have been increased gradually, which, when combined with statutory holidays and accumulation of sick leave and discretionary time off, amount to as much as one-tenth of the total working time for employees. When account is taken of all the time that employed people are not at work for one reason or another, the average work week shrinks to no more than twenty-eight hours! This is only about 1,460 hours of work per year! Considering that there are 8,760 hours in the year, the 1,460 hours represent only 16 per cent of the total time at our disposal. This would not in itself be adequate evidence that we are increasingly becoming accustomed to work less, except for the increasing pressures by employee organizations for still fewer hours of work, more statutory holidays, longer vacations, more cumulative sick leave, and greater flexibility in work scheduling to allow for more frequent times off work.

Therefore, the problem is not with technology doing more of the work and producing more of the goods and services and people having less work; the problem is *the distribution* of the available work among the people who want to work. Some people work many more hours than they should; some work many more hours than they need to; others work much less than they would like to; and still others do not work at all and would like to have some work. There is no reason, for example, that some physicians should work fifty, sixty, or seventy hours per week, when many of the functions they perform can be performed with equal efficiency and effectiveness by other health-related occupations that require much less education and training. An efficient distribution of work functions in the health-care field will result in an entirely different mix of health-care occupations and in a significantly different distribution of the work at significantly lower costs. Similarly, there is no reason that some lawyers, accountants, engineers, and other professionals, who create and control the amount of work to be done in relation to individual contracts and projects, should allocate to themselves and their associates large amounts of work involving long hours. If they were less greedy wealth accumulators, they would distribute the work downward among larger numbers of people.

Discussions on work sharing[9] as a potential partial solution to the problem of excessive involuntary unemployment have focused on low- and middle-level work activities and occupations that provide low and average incomes. The sharing of work and wages at levels of work that provide average incomes will redistribute work but reduce the living standards of people who struggle with relatively low standards. That is not efficient work redistribution, and it results in inequitable distribution of incomes. Efficiency in work distribution and equity in the distribution of work-related incomes will not be achieved through the redistribution of the normal workload performed by the average worker. It will only be achieved through downward distribution of work from those who create and control the volume of work, allocate to themselves above normal amounts of work, and earn above normal incomes. It will be achieved, for example, when the highly successful, "hard-working" insurance representative, real estate representative, lawyer, doctor, engineer, accountant, or whoever allocates some of his or her lower-level work functions to assistants. But for such a system to evolve, a new ethic that places less emphasis on the accumulation of wealth will have to prevail.

Notes

1. This is examined in considerable detail by David Brody and David C. Buchanan in "Information Technology and the Experience of Work," paper presented at a European Economic Community Conference on the Information Society in Dublin, Ireland, November 18-20, 1981.
2. This is examined in considerable detail in Chapter 7.
3. Rauf Gönenc, "Software – A New Industry," *The OEDC Observer*, No. 131 (November, 1984), pp. 20-23.
4. Nuala Swords-Isherwood, "Women in British Engineering," in W. Faulkner and E. Arnold, eds., *Smothered by Invention – Technology in Women's Lives* (London: Pluto Press, 1985), pp. 80-81.
5. Bruna Teso and Salomon Wald, "Government Policy and Biotechnology: Four Key Issues," *The OEDC Observer*, No. 131 (November, 1984), pp. 16-19.
6. A good examination of the functional activities of the "housewife occupation" will be found in Barbara R. Bergmann, "The Economic Risks of Being a Housewife," *American Economic Review* (May, 1981), pp. 81-85.
7. Jonathan Gershuny, *After Industrial Society? The Emerging Self-Service Economy* (London: Macmillan, 1978).
8. A. Oakley, *Housewife: High Value and Low Cost* (Hammondsworth: Penguin, 1976), p. 4.
9. Fred Best, *Work Sharing: Issues, Policy Options and Prospects* (Kalamazoo, Michigan: The Upjohn Institute, 1981).

5

Occupational Distribution of Women

The distribution of women in the labour force has the shape of a short pyramid with a very broad base: the largest number are involved in activities related to various forms of communication – clerical, secretarial, organizational, transactional (cashiers, tellers); the next largest group are involved in retailing, catering, and general services; next are a fairly large number in para-professional, supervisory, and technical occupations; managerial and professional women make up the next group; and at the top are the relatively few women who have made their way into the highest levels of the judiciary, government, industry, the arts, and institutions. Graphically, the structure takes the shape of Figure 5.1.

By contrast, the occupational distribution of men in the labour force has taken the shape of a barrel, with about equal numbers at the bottom and the top and the majority concentrated in the middle in supervisory, technical, para-professional, professional, and managerial occupations.

Over the past two decades the occupational structure of women has been undergoing some notable changes: the occupational mix of those entering the labour force has been significantly different from the mix of the overall structure. Increasing numbers of women have entered professional occupations, have pursued educational and training programs qualifying them for high-level organizational and supervisory activities, and have advanced to managerial and administrative positions.[1]

Figure 5.1
Occupational Distribution of Women

Implications of Pyramid Structure for Employment

The perception of the occupational structure and of employment in the form of a pyramid has important implications for employment preparation, employment, progression in employment, and accommodation to changes in employment. A pyramid is a vertical structure, starting from a broad base and narrowing as one ascends toward the peak. This imposes two constraints on those working within the structure: first, advancement in employment is limited to vertical progression; second, the range of opportunities decreases rapidly as one progresses toward the top. In this context, it is quite understandable why those at the bottom levels of the pyramid should be apprehensive about the possibility of technology, for example, reducing the range of employment opportunities. If movement is only upward, and opportunities at higher levels are fewer and require higher qualifications, where are they to go? If secretarial and clerical positions decrease significantly, where are they to go within a pyramid with decreasing positions at higher levels, which require different preparation?

In reality, employment structures are not as limiting as is commonly assumed: occupational groups and employments are not rigidly compartmentalized; upward progression is not limited to a few steps; and in many occupations there are many opportunities for horizontal progression. The shift in employment from goods production to the production of services, for example, increased the range of employment activities and spread out the employment structure. The structure of employment remains stratified vertically, but the expanded range of employment activities has increased the number of levels of employment and the number of positions within each level. As a result, there are now more opportunities for vertical and horizontal mobility than there were when most of the labour force was engaged in producing goods. This is easily attested by an examination of the employment structure of any services-producing enterprise in health care, banking, government, transportation, or utilities. A vice-president of the Prudential Insurance Company has said: "Fifteen years ago we had a pyramid-shaped staff, with large numbers at entry-level clerical jobs at the bottom. As technology was introduced, the shape has altered so that the pyramid looks like an onion or a football. We may be going toward a diamond."[2] Many of the low-level jobs in filing, invoicing, record-keeping are gone; but the number of supervisors, advisers, counsellors, and administrators has increased.

Notwithstanding the note of optimism in the foregoing, there is legitimate concern about the accommodation of those at the lowest levels of the pyramid if expectations were to be confirmed that modern technology will reduce significantly the number of employment positions at those levels. What would a clerk do if clerical positions were to be reduced significantly? Vertical progression is unlikely, and horizontal mobility may be limited to the few clerical positions related to computer operations.

Also, even though the number of levels in the pyramid has increased, they are nevertheless limited. This limitation imposes a limit on the upward progress of women, particularly in periods of limited growth when enterprises fail to expand. At such times upward progress becomes limited to emerging vacancies from retirement and promotions. But, considering the vertical nature of the employment structure and the decreasing number of positions as one ascends toward the top, at each level there are a number of candidates for each higher-level position becoming vacant. A potential for conflict exists between men in positions of advantage for upward mobility and women aspiring to upward mobility but standing at less advantageous positions within the pyramid.

Knowledge and the Occupational Structure

One of the most important developments contributing to the broadening of the occupational structure over the past century is the phenomenal increase in knowledge. Every field of endeavour, from the arts and humanities to the engineering sciences, the health sciences, and the social sciences, has experienced an explosion in knowledge.

The relationship between knowledge and occupations is in the level of knowledge and range of work functions associated with individual occupations. As the level of knowledge increases and the range of work functions expands, it becomes necessary to specialize in small parts of it, which is reflected in the division and subdivision of individual occupations. Consider, for example, engineering, medicine, nursing, law, accounting, and other occupations that experienced increases in knowledge in their areas of activity: there are dozens of engineering specializations, and a glance through the Yellow Pages of the telephone directory will reveal more than fifty medical specializations. There was a time not very long ago when the medical doctor attended to all health problems, including surgery, the delivery of babies, the preparation of medications, the prescription of special diets, and so on. Over time, as knowledge of health expanded, physicians specialized in the multitude of higher levels of medical problems and passed downward some of their work functions to other occupations – to nurses, respiratory technicians, pharmacists, and others. Also, the recognition that the maintenance of health involved much more than what physical medicine could offer resulted in an expanded role for the nurse and the emergence of clinical psychologists, medical social workers (who really are health social workers), occupational therapists, dieticians, and many others. At the same time, efficiency considerations in the use of specialized resources resulted in the transfer of clerical and housekeeping functions from nurses to ward clerks and ward maids.[3]

Such is the consequence of the increase in knowledge in all areas of occupational activity: occupations whose knowledge becomes redundant disappear, while occupations whose knowledge expands divide and subdivide into additional occupations. Medical specialists in tuberculosis, polio, diphtheria, and small pox have almost disappeared; the number of specialists in surgery, diseases of the heart, cancer, etc. have increased substantially.[4]

There is no reason we should not experience the same occupational developments in relation to the vast range of work activities to which computers and telecommunications technology are applied. What has happened and continues to happen is that our knowledge of the application of computer and telecommunications technology has been expanding rapidly, and with it there is a continuous expansion in new approaches to the performance of work. These will be manifested in new occupations and employments. The only obstacle to the conversion of new approaches to the performance of work into new employment opportunities is the failure of the economy to expand, and the associated decline in the ability of the economy to support more people at the existing living standard and to ensure an increasing living standard. As long as application of the increase in knowledge results in increases in productivity and in higher national income, the economy will have the capacity to support increments in employment. In other words, the increase in knowledge makes necessary the division and subdivision of existing occupations into additional occupations and the creation of new occupations, while the increase in income makes possible the employment of the additional and new occupations.

A good example of this relationship between income and employment is found in a comment by the comedian Jonathan Winters on the number of people involved in the production of his show. He expressed nostalgia for the period when comedians wrote most of their material and improvised in the course of the performance. Now they have directors, writers, censors with law degrees, and scores of consultants and have to follow the script lest they offend some group in society. What does this change mean? It can be interpreted to mean that social attitudes have changed over time, consumers have become more knowledgeable and more sophisticated in their expectations, and minority groups in society expect the same recognition and respect as accorded the majority. But there is another meaning as well, an economic meaning: the general increase in productivity and incomes increased demand for higher quality of goods and services, including entertainment. The production of good comedy involves the employment of more people, higher costs, and higher prices. Even so, the number of high-priced comedians has increased, and the number of producers, writers, censors, and so on multiplied manyfold – all because people are able to pay. Television networks are able to charge high prices to advertisers, who in turn charge higher prices to their customers. In countries where incomes are relatively low, comedians continue to produce their own material and continue to improvise as they perform.

It is possible, of course, to create additional employment without an increase in income, but it will involve income redistribution. Depending on the nature and degree of redistribution, the period of time over which it takes place, and its incentive/disincentive effects, it may result in a decrease in living standards. A case in point is the voluntary income redistribution that took place with the introduction of lotteries. It is estimated that more than 10,000 full-time job equivalents were created over time in activities related to the system – in the design and printing of tickets, the sale of tickets, promotions, and administration. In addition, employment was created by the expenditures of those employed in the system and by the expenditures of lottery winners. But this is only one side of the equation, which is the expenditure of money taken from people by means of painless taxation. On the other side are the expenditures of the people from whom the money is taken, who now have less money to spend on other goods and services, which means that the jobs created in the production of those other goods and services are no longer created. What has happened in effect is that the redistribution of incomes and expenditures resulted simply in the redistribution of employment. Instead of being employed in a department store, the clerk is now employed selling lottery tickets.

Redistributions of income and expenditure largely redistribute employment, unless the income being redistributed had been dormant in unused savings or had been spent outside the country without reciprocal expenditure from outside the country. Yet even when redistribution results in a net increase in employment, that is a one-phase result: when the redistribution is completed, the employment creation will come to an end. The same logic applies to distributions of available work among increasing numbers of job-seekers, which is often referred to as job-sharing. A common argument of those who favour such proposals is that the reduction in hours of work will result in an increase in average productivity and incomes, which will create additional employment. But this, too, like the employment effect of income redistribution, is a one-phase development. It will end with the end of the redistribution in available work. As soon as total income and the volume of work reach a given level and remain thereafter at that level, additional employment will not be created without sacrifice in living standards. The continuous creation of employment to accommodate an increasing working-age population and sustain an increasing standard of living is conditional on continuous economic growth and rising per capita income.

The relationship between knowledge and employment brings to attention the importance of the acquisition of new knowledge by groups in society, such as women, which have been excluded from participation or whose participation in desirable occupations has been limited. The only certain way that women, like other discriminated groups, can secure employment in critical areas of economic and social activity is through the acquisition of the new knowledge. Preparation for employment through the acquisition of long-established knowledge faces the risk of competition from those who have long had the knowledge and from those who acquired the new knowledge. Whereas preparation for employment with the acquisition of new knowledge gives promise that the new knowledge will expand and thereby result in increasing specialization and the creation of new occupations. Whether total employment increases, remains the same, or decreases, the distribution of occupations will change in favour of those with new knowledge.

The application of new knowledge to instruments, processes, and the organization of work has implications for the nature and range of work activities, the conditions under which the work activities are performed, and often for the nature of skills required for the performance of the work. Technology is not in itself deterministic in its effects; whatever effects it has may well be the result of what designers and developers of the technology incorporated into it. The question arises whether the technology used by women would have been designed and developed differently if designers and developers were women rather than men. It is often asserted that "Women experience paid work differently from men and these differences are intensified by new technology because its development, introduction and use are largely out to their control."[5] If such assertions are substantially valid, then women could benefit if more women were to carry out research in the development of new knowledge and were to engage in the design and development of products, instruments, and processes.

In summary, although the evidence to date is not adequate for a definitive statement on the nature, range, and level of skills that will emerge from the ongoing technological revolution, there is a well-established general principle on the matter: *the nature, range, and level of skills are functions of the level of knowledge that is applied to productive activity.* Historically, increasing knowledge has resulted in increasing specialization shown in changes in the nature of work at different levels of the work process, the subdivision of occupations in different classifications and occupational categories, and changes in the organization of work. There is no reason that the same outcomes should not materialize from the increase in knowledge associated with the advent and application of microelectronic instruments and processes. In fact, an examination of the changes in the occupational structure over the past twenty years will attest to this development: new occupations emerged, which over time divided and subdivided into scores of specializations; existing occupations at all levels acquired new knowledge, which in most instances raised the level of their work skills; and the nature of work generally has increased to a higher level than it was at the inception of computers and computer-related technology.

The changes that have taken place in computer programming and the specialization of programmer-analyst exemplify this. Initially, the occupation was a general one, not unlike that of engineer or physician of many decades ago. With the increasing sophistication in computer applications to diverse activities it has become necessary for programmers to specialize. Similarly, the work functions of existing occupations within offices have changed drastically – in finance, in retail trade, in consultative services to individuals and enterprises, and in educational and health services. Everywhere there has been an increase in the level of operational knowledge. The capacity to store and access information in different forms and configurations has broadened the range of knowledge of all who use computers and computer-related instruments and processes. Almost imperceptibly, secretaries using word processors, video-display terminals, and other instruments have become in effect research associates, administrative associates, and information specialists. *Therefore, the evidence to date suggests a general upgrading in knowledge and skills,* which is consistent with the historical outcome of increases in knowledge.

Artificial Intelligence

To most people the concept of artificial intelligence conjures up frightening implications – the displacement of physiological human intelligence by electronic intelligence. But artificial intelligence has important implications for the preservation and dissemination of knowledge and for employment creation. It provides an opportunity to preserve and disseminate knowledge that otherwise may be wasted and to preserve and use a capital investment in knowledge that otherwise would disappear.

Such knowledge and investment are in the work experience of high-level specialists in various fields of work. In the past such expertise was passed on from generation to generation through the apprenticeship system, where the apprentice worked and often lived with the master. Expertise not passed on to an apprentice died with the death of the expert. Some expert knowledge has, of course, been recorded and transmitted from generation to generation through articles and books, but much on-the-job experience has been lost by sudden death or by the failure to put that knowledge in writing: the steelworker who "knew" when the steel bar was ready by the colour of the glow; the geologist-prospector who has been highly successful on "hunches";

the scientist who "saw" a possibility that thousands of other scientists did not.

The computer and "knowledge" engineers can now assemble that expert knowledge, organize it, and put it in usable form. Through painstaking interviews of such experts, knowledge engineers (software writers) convert subjective judgements into rules and probabilities the computer can receive, process, and evaluate. Out of the visual pictures that only the expert can see, the odour that only the expert can detect, and the sound the expert can discern come a wide range of probabilities, some quantifiable and some not, some with theoretical validity and some defying accepted theoretical postulates, some emerging as pure chance unlikely to happen again and some showing consistent patterns. The end result is knowledge of alternatives to be considered, possibilities to be examined and tested, outcomes to be verified.

The implications of all these for employment cannot be identified precisely and quantified, but it can be said with certainty that they are likely to be positive. The certainty that they are likely to be positive is founded on their effect on knowledge, which is positive and expansive. It is well established, of course, that there is a positive relationship between the expansion in knowledge and employment.

Effect of Computer Technology on Employment Structure

We have noted that one of the explanations for the increased number of women in the labour market is the mechanization of the home, which reduced the demand for labour in the household economy, thereby leaving excess labour supply to be offered in the market economy. It follows from this that when we consider the effect of computers on the employment of women, we must look at the application of computing processes everywhere – at home, at leisure activities, wherever human activity is affected.

We have identified three groups of activities: work that relates to home and family; market work for pay or profit; and leisure. The work related to home and family has, over time, become generally capital-intensive – washing machines (clothes and dishes), vacuum cleaners, electro-mechanical kitchen implements, and factory-prepared foods. With the advent of electronic and communications technologies, the capital intensity has been increased by the introduction of microwave ovens, cable services providing access to wide-ranging programs for family education, information, and entertainment, and computers that centralize all household information. These and many other ongoing additions to household capital structures have reduced further and will continue to reduce the time allocated to household work, notwithstanding Jonathan Gershuny's thesis that many of these technologies are largely transforming the household from a consumption unit to a production unit.[6]

From an economic standpoint, the increasing capital intensity of the household has been in response to the general lack of division of labour in household activities and the resultant inefficiency in operations.[7] It was simply not possible to achieve reasonable levels of efficiency and effectiveness in the performance of the many tasks involved in the management and functional operation of the average family household when most management and work functions were performed by one person and when the person involved commonly assumed the responsibilities with very limited educational training in them. Clearly, assistance was needed, and to the extent that it was not forthcoming from within the household on a continuous basis it was sought in capital substitutes and complements. The washing and drying of clothes was taken over by machines, and housecleaning was assisted by vacuum cleaners and by a variety of cleaning ingredients and accessories.

The introduction of instruments and products in household work increased the efficiency of household operations generally, but the basic problem of inadequate division of labour in the household economy remains. It is logical, then, to expect that as long as the operation and management of the family household remain largely in the hands of relatively unskilled individuals, the quest will continue for more capital instruments to help in the work. Furthermore, with increasing levels of education among women and their increasing participation in the market economy in specialized work that reflects their education and training, the performance of menial household activities becomes increasingly personally demeaning, and generally rather costly.

In economic terms, the opportunity cost of household activities increases directly with the value of services provided in the market economy by an increasingly educated population of women. Therefore, one can expect continuing efforts to reduce the time allocated to menial household activities: computerization of kitchen implements and factory-prepared foods to reduce the time needed to prepare meals; computerization of household operations to reduce the time involved in planning, budgeting, and general management; computerized and modulated educational and recreational programs to reduce the time allocation and increase the quality of educational and recreational activities. All this will create surplus time in the household economy, which will allow for more time in the market economy or in leisure activities. It is important to note, though, that the expertise gained in the performance of household activities has limited market value. Therefore, the time vacated from household activities cannot be transferred to market activities without the acquisition of knowledge and skills employed in the market economy.

There is, then, the important question of what will happen to employment in the market economy. Will the market economy continue to absorb the surplus time generated in the household economy? It did in the past three decades or so because of the rapid growth in the economy and the expansion in service activities in offices, in retail trade, in financial institutions of all kinds and real estate, in the myriad services provided by the three levels of government and government boards and agencies, in health and education, in personal services, and in all sorts of services to business. An important employment-related characteristic of all these services is that they were largely labour-intensive. Either because appropriate technology did not exist or because labour was cheaper, most of the work done in them was done largely by labour.

With the advent of computer technology the service market economy is becoming as capital-intensive as the service household economy. But, unlike the household economy, the service market economy is expansive – the quantity and range of activities has expanded at a faster rate than the rate of increase in capital-initiated efficiency. As a result, employment in it has continued to increase. Whether this will continue with the increasing integration of computer and telecommunications systems remains uncertain. There is no doubt that employment in some activities will continue to expand and that some new employment activities will emerge and expand as well; and there is no doubt, too, that employment in some other areas will contract and in some others even disappear.[8] What is in doubt is what will happen on balance. Perhaps we should look at what is happening in the office, since more than half of the women employed in service activities are engaged in varying forms of office work.

Employment in the Office

The advent of technology appropriate for many of the activities performed in offices, and a perception of offices as relatively inefficient, provided stimulus for substantial investment in office equipment over the past two decades. Computers, video-display terminals, word processors, laser printers, electronic mail, and many other instruments and processes have changed radically the nature and organization of office work. All of this change has been for the purpose of increasing productivity and reducing office costs.[9]

The result to date is positive in relation to productivity in activities where the technology has been applied, uncertain in relation to overall office productivity, and equally uncertain in relation to office costs. Productivity has increased substantially in activities that relate to the gathering, recording, manipulation, and communication of information, in the administration of payroll, billing, accounts payable and receivable, in the management of inventory, as well as in the activities involving typing, printing, charting, reproducing, and the like. But many of these activities are no longer performed in the office; they will be found instead in the computer centre or the information systems department. As a result, it is rather difficult to determine what has happened to overall productivity and costs in the office itself. What the office does is increasingly linked to or integrated with other parts of the organization. The capacity and efficiency of the computer systems will bear on the efficiency of the office, and so will the demands of the system units linked to it.

The output of what is being produced in the average office appears to have gone up substantially, and so has the output per person employed in the office, but there is considerable doubt whether the output of final office products has increased as substantially. The capacity of office systems to produce output rapidly at the press of a key appears to have created a rather casual attitude about what is produced and how much is produced. Getting a copy of this or that appears to have become more of a routine than asking a question. Similarly, more work appears to be produced in preliminary form, followed by many revisions and amendments. In other words, the final reports may not have changed significantly, but the background information entering into their preparation has increased manyfold and the reports themselves have gone through more revisions than under the old system, with many more sophisticated tables and charts, better headings, and better type.

Furthermore, the computer-based systems that make possible an increase in office output and an increase in the sophistication of the output involve a significant increase in the numbers of specialized workers in offices – lawyers, accountants, analysts, programmers, financial specialists, economists, statisticians, mathematicians, engineers, administrators, managers, and co-ordinators.[10] These are high-level occupations commanding significantly higher salaries than the occupations that are displaced, and their work does not lend itself to easy identification, definition, and measurement. It is much easier to identify and measure the work of clerks and typists than the work of administrators, financial analysts, computer programmers and analysts, economists, lawyers, and their like.

When work cannot be identified, defined, and measured, it cannot be controlled. The tendency, then, is to create work to fill the time, which is easily done at meetings, in travel, at conferences, and through other forms of verbal and audio communication. The picture that emerges from this increasingly computer-based office organization may not be as cost-efficient as its designers and propagators assert. The system will have to generate a significant increase in output to offset the payments to high-salaried occupational groups employed in it and the cost of capital equipment that seems to have a very short operational life. A sceptical jury continues to struggle with this.

The expectation that computerization of the office will increase productivity in the office and reduce office costs is based on experiences with goods-producing processes. Whether such experiences are relevant for service-producing processes remains to be determined. The outputs of goods-producing processes are precise and quantifiable – thousands of widgets, millions of pairs of shoes. It can easily be determined how many can be produced per hour, and how many more or less will be produced if certain changes were to be introduced in the production processes. Such is the case also for some office activities, such as typing.

But for most other office activities, particularly those performed at the supervisory, professional, and management levels, such specification is not possible. The activities performed by such people are various and expansive: identifying issues, developing markets, initiating projects, co-ordinating activities, evaluating outcomes and performances, developing and maintaining relationships, searching, collecting, and developing information, etc. There is almost no limit to the work that can be created in relation to such activities. The employment records of enterprises, governments, and institutions suggest that such work and the employment associated with it are a function of the capacity to pay. In other words, given ability to pay, work can be created and employment will increase, regardless of the quantity and nature of technology employed in the office.

When computers and computer-related instruments were first introduced in offices, predictions put all office occupations at high risk. Clerks and typists were singled out as particularly vulnerable. Yet, instead of the expected widespread decline in employment and in employment opportunities in offices, total employment in the general "clerical" classification actually increased from 752,000 in 1960 to 1,928,000 in 1986, or by 156 per cent. The employment of women in that same classification tripled from 467,000 in 1960 to 1,537,000 in 1986 – by 229 per cent! Even in more recent years, when office technology became more widespread and more integrated, employment has continued to increase. In the clerical classification, total employment increased from 1,877,000 in 1982 to 1,928,000 in 1986, and the employment of women from 1,480,000 in 1982 to 1,537,000 in 1986.

This reveals an important general principle in the relationship between technology and employment. The general principle is that the rate of change in total employment depends on the rate of increase in productivity relative to the rate of increase in demand for that which is produced. If demand for the output increases faster than the rate of increase in productivity, employment will increase; if demand increases less than the increase in productivity, employment will decrease. Employment in individual occupations may decrease; but overall employment in the production process will behave in accordance with the general principle. In the case of office work, the total volume of "clerical" work increased, to more than offset the increase in output associated with the introduction of the technology.

In addition to this, the computer technology expanded the range of office services into activities which, although necessary, were too costly to carry out with pre-computer methods. The preparation of comprehensive reports, tables, graphics, and data analysis are good examples. This expansion in the range of office activities created substantial employment opportunities. And there are, of course, the many newly created technology-related office occupations of programmers, systems analysts, computer operators, input clerks, output clerks, tape librarians, and others. Clearly, predictions about the employment and output effects of new technologies are hazardous to one's professional reputation. The lesson from all of this for all of us is to examine with care all of the assumptions that underlie the predictions.[11] In relation to the future, a recent United States study found no persuasive evidence of any significant decline in clerical jobs, either as a result of further improvements in technology or as a result of improvements in productivity in the office.[12]

In summary, the record of employment changes in the office over the past twenty-five years indicates that employment in some office occupations decreased, but that decrease was more than offset by increases in employment in other occupations, including newly created technology-related occupations. As a result, the overall employment in the office increased substantially. In other words, overall employment increased, and the occupational structure changed rather significantly.

In addition to changing the structure of employment and the occupational mix, technology has changed the traditional perception of some office jobs as "women's" jobs. Increasing numbers of men, at all levels of the occupational structure, are now found at the keyboards of word processors and computer terminals. Only a few years ago the issue was debated whether men would be willing to perform what were perceived as typing functions associated with female secretaries.

The Erosion of Gender Characteristics in Office Jobs

There are important implications for the employment of both men and women in the erosion of gender characteristics in office jobs. Competition between men and women in the marketplace is likely to increase. As long as most women were concentrated in jobs associated with women and most men were in those associated with men, competition between men and women was limited. With the erosion of such traditional associations and the opening-up of employments to both men and women, competition will intensify.

The outcome of the competitive struggles seems to favour both men and women: women will probably increase their representation in the professional employments in which they have made significant inroads in recent years, but they will likely lose ground in some other areas of the expanding information economy. The reason for this is found in ongoing changes in employment: while women are seeking to preserve the jobs they now have and to get access to higher-level jobs traditionally dominated by men, employment opportunities in some of the industries that traditionally employed large numbers of men have been steadily declining. Men who would have been employed in skilled trades, on the railways, in mining, in steel, and in a score of manufacturing processes will now seek employment in the expanding information and services sectors formerly dominated by women. In the 1976-86 decade employment in services increased 23.8 per cent, in clerical and sales activities by 5.7 per cent, in medicine and health, 27.3 per cent, in teaching and sciences, 20.8 per cent, in management, 110.6 per cent, for a total increase in the so-called white-collar jobs of 23.7 per cent; in the same period employment in the so-called blue-collar jobs decreased by 6.5 per – cent down 14.6 per cent in processing and machinery, down 17 per cent in construction, and down 1.8 per cent in materials handling. Only transport equipment operation and product fabricating, assembling, and repairing recorded increases.[13] The workers who would have sought employment in processing, construction, and trades will in future seek training and search for employment in alternative activities. Most of the alternative activities in which employment is expanding are the activities dominated heretofore by women.

But the entry of increasing numbers of men in employments dominated by women could have significant benefits to women: historically, the entry of men in such employments brought improvements in the terms and conditions of employment – jobs became upgraded, with associated improvements in pay and benefits. If history were to become current reality, we should witness the upgrading of jobs in the office, which in fact is attested by the changing mix of occupational classifications in the office over the past decade or two.

The mix will continue to change, of course, as new instruments and production processes change the range of functions performed within individual employment classifications. In relation to the employment of women and the levels at which women are employed the critical question is what work functions are dropped, what are changed, what are added, and who is assigned to the higher-level functions. We noted earlier that the occupational structure is vertical and hierarchical. Each occupation in the structure has a range of work functions, which in many work situations overlap in varying degrees with the work of occupations above and below them. The secure occupations are those that control the work functions associated with them and at the same time exercise some influence on the work functions performed by the occupations associated with them in work. If there is erosion in the overlapping range of functions, the losers will be those who occupy the subordinate positions. Consider, for example, the overlapping work functions of doctors, nurses, and nursing assistants. Erosion in the overlapping ranges will affect nurses negatively in relation to doctors, and nursing assistants in relation to nurses.

Computer Effects on the Organization of Office Work

Computers and telecommunications technologies have a number of characteristics that will affect the organization of office work. Three of them are relevant to women: one is the pervasiveness of the technologies, which means they are appropriate for all kinds of office-related work; the second is their capacity to interact with one another; and the third is the capacity to communicate information and access information in large quantities, over long distances, at a very high speed.

These characteristics are shifting the locus of efficiency in work organizations from concentration to spatial dispersion. The use of computer surrogates, and the opportunity to access employment-related work at will, will change the pattern of work from "time specific" to continuous, in the sense of not ending at the end of what has come to be "a day's work." Given such an expansion in the scope of work activity, it will become increasingly difficult to continue with the existing rigidities in work time, hours of work, and place of work. This suggests that computers and telecommunications technologies contain the technical and scientific potential to foster a new organization of work, characterized by flexibility in relation to when people work, the number of hours they work in any given day, and where they perform the activities expected of them. One observer of the emerging trends concluded that the technology "will produce an increasing overlapping between the two temporal cycles of everyday life – work and outside work."[14] There is evidence of increasing income-producing work being done from homes with the advent of the personal computer, which undoubtedly will increase further as prices of personal computers decrease further and as these become increasingly linked to information centres and to employment-related mainframes.[15] According to Toffler, jobs will increasingly shift "out of factories and office ... and right back where they came from originally: the home."[16]

Toffler's assertion gives a high degree of determinism to technology. In his perspective, technology not only makes possible alternative forms of work organization but also dictates that the alternative forms be put into effect. History reveals a different reality. The possibility of dispersion in work activity existed long before the introduction of computers; yet centralization, not dispersion, has been the general trend. People can perform many work activities at home with equal and even greater efficiency than at their places of employment. Yet, these people are required to report at a place of employment, which suggests that centralization of work activity in places of employment may be social and organizational in origin, not necessarily dictated by the requirements of the work processes.

The possibility that one can, from distance, access information from a system and input information into a system used by associates in work should be viewed as a significant advantage to women. Notwithstanding the concerns expressed by some women's groups that such possibilities will burden women further by making them both full-time mothers and homemakers and full-time workers, many working women will probably welcome the opportunity to work from home. Existing working relationships dictate that such women sever their employment for the duration of their stay at home.

The severance of employment relationships has placed women at a disadvantage: depending on the length of the interruption, productivity may be affected, some retraining may become necessary, and working relationships may have changed, which may require adjustment to new environments. The computer telecommunications systems make it possible to remain in continuous contact with the "production process" since much of the work involved in the production and processing of information is not space-specific in the nature of, for example, working in construction, driving a bus, or working on an assembly line. Given some flexibility in the assignment of responsibilities, it is possible to employ people in independent as well as collaborative work without having them concentrated in one physical space. The systems allow for remote input, manipulation, and retrieval of text and graphics; permit the remote interaction of computer-controlled typesetting of documents to be produced; and make possible continuous interaction among collaborators in work dispersed over space. In this context, one can be away from the office, yet continue to participate in the work of the office. Such continuity should ameliorate the discriminatory practices founded on negative expectations associated with entry-exit patterns of employment.

Patterns in the Employment of Women

We have noted that the employment of women is characterized by entry/exit, re-entry/re-exit patterns, with varying periods of interruption. Although both the number and duration of interruptions have decreased in recent years, the decrease has coincided with some significant changes in the structure of employment and in the functional content of jobs. As a result, women continue to face serious adjustment problems upon re-entry into the labour market. In periods of relative stability in the structure of the economy and in the techno-structure of production processes, the nature and range of work functions tend to remain relatively stable. In such work conditions, re-employment after a period of interruption in employment does not present any serious adjustment problem. The situation is different in periods of change in production processes, in technology, and in the organization of work. On re-entry they find their skills eroded and lack recent experience in new processes and new equipment, and they are at a disadvantage in competition with young new entrants who offer up-to-date knowledge and skills at entry-level wages.[17] In addition, separation from the market over prolonged periods tends to sever employment relationships and contacts. Upon re-entry one tends to find oneself with limited information on opportunities. Longitudinal surveys in the United States indicate that one of every three women experiences a period of unemployment upon re-entry because the women lack job information, because they tend to over-value their services, and because their job expectations are at variance with employer assessments of their potential.[18]

Interruptions in employment, whether voluntary or involuntary, have implications also for advancement within the employment structure. Even where contractual provisions exist for the reinstatement of employees to their jobs on return to work, as in the case of maternity leaves, reinstatement is commonly to the old positions. While such arrangements provide protection against demotions and reductions in pay, they also leave such employees behind those who moved to higher positions. Therefore, although they may not suffer absolute reductions in pay, they may well suffer relative reductions. Herbert Parnes has found that interruptions in employment lead to long-term reductions in earning capacity, especially among younger women.[19]

Whether integrated computer and telecommunications systems will reduce the historical disadvantages of interruptions in employment remains to be determined. Certainly the link of the home computer to the computer at work makes it possible to remain in continuous contact with the work processes and to interact with work associates. In other words, physical separation from the work environment need not mean discontinuity in work.

But we do not really know what will happen to work processes, what qualifications will be required for continuous involvement in them, and what occupational structure will emerge in future. Three sets of questions exist to which answers are yet to be provided. One relates to *the nature of work*. What will the technological infrastructure be like in the office, in educational and health institutions, in service activities? What kind of work organization will evolve? What occupational divisions and subdivisions will emerge? What kind of work functions will people perform? What will be the interface between people and the technology? Without answers to these questions, all statements on occupations and employment are largely speculative, even though founded on trends and analysis.

The second question relates to *qualifications for employment*. It is not possible to determine the nature of specific qualifications people would need for continuous participation without knowing first the nature of the technological infrastructure in which they will work and the nature of interface they will have with the technology. For example, most of the jobs that have emerged around computer operations require much less knowledge and skill than was projected two or three decades ago.

The third question also relates to the qualifications for employment, but it *is concerned with whether the technology will neutralize distance, time, continuity, and spatial concentration.* If the result is dispersion in the organization of work, as Toffler has suggested, and if the work can be performed any time, from any place, the profiles of people will be neutralized. The ability to do the work will be the employment-determining criterion, not whether the individual is able to report to a place of work, whether the individual is able to remain at the place of work without interruption for certain hours per day, day per week, and so on, or whether the individual is man, woman, young, old, married with children, black, white, or yellow.

The answers to these questions will come gradually, as we move toward the integrated and interactive computer telecommunications systems in which computer surrogates will interact with one another and, increasingly, perform many of the functions we now perform. But a surrogate is by definition a deputy that will perform those functions it is deputized to perform. This, of course, raises yet another question that relates to the creation of employment and the use of the fruits of employment. Is it possible that in the new technological system most of the routine menial work will be performed by such surrogates? In such case, over time the base of the occupational pyramid will be increasingly occupied by surrogates.

Notes

1. For evidence of this trend, see Chapter 7.
2. Richard I. Kirkland, Jr., "Are Service Jobs Good Jobs?," *Economic Impact*, No. 52 (1985), p. 20.
3. For the nature of distribution in occupations in hospitals, libraries, and retail and wholesale trade as a result of the introduction of computer technology, see Steven Globerman, *The Adoption of Computer Technology in Selected Canadian Service Industries* (Ottawa: Economic Council of Canada, 1981).
4. Joseph Schumpeter characterized "technological change" as the process of creative destruction. *Capitalism, Socialism and Democracy* (London: Allen & Unwin, 1943).
5. N. Swords-Isherwood *et al.*, "Technical Change and Its Effects on Employment Opportunities for Women," in P. Marstrand, ed., *New Technology and the Future of Work and Skills* (London: Frances Pinter, 1984), p. 205.
6. Jonathan Gershuny, *After Industrial Society? The Emerging Self-*

Service Economy (London: Macmillan, 1978).

7. For a good examination of this issue, see Barbara Bergmann, "The Economic Risks of Being a Housewife," *American Economic Review: Papers and Proceedings* (May, 1981), pp. 81-85.

8. Economic Council of Canada, *Innovations and Jobs in Canada* (Ottawa, 1987).

9. John J. Connell, "Office of the 1980's: Productivity Impact," *Business Week*, February 18, 1980.

10. Paul A. Strassman, "The Office of the Future: Information Management for the New Age," *Technology Review* (December/January, 1980), pp. 54-65.

11. A good presentation on the subject matter will be found in Jerome A. Mark, "Impact of Technological Change on Labour," paper presented at the National Conference on the Impacts of Technological Change on the Workplace, St. Louis, Missouri, June, 1979.

12. H.A. Hunt and T.L. Hunt, *Clerical Employment and Technological Change* (Kalamazoo, Michigan: The Upjohn Institute, 1986).

13. Statistics Canada, *The Labour Force*, December, 1976 (Table 40), and December, 1986 (Table 71).

14. Chantal de Gautnay, "Leisure and Cultural Activities in the Information Society," EEC Conference on the Information Society, Dublin, Ireland, November 18-20, 1981.

15. Alvin Toffler examines this issue in *The Third Wave* (New York: Bantam Books, 1981), p. 194.

16. *Ibid.*

17. See D.M. Lilien, "Structural Shifts in Cyclical Unemployment," *Journal of Political Economy* (August, 1982), pp. 77-93

18. See Ethel B. Jones, *Determinants of Female Re-Entrant Employment* (Kalamazoo, Michigan: The Upjohn Institute, 1983); S. Kaliski "Why Must Unemployment Remain So High?," *Canadian Public Policy* (June, 1984), pp. 127-41

19. Herbert S. Parnes, *Unemployment Experience of Individuals Over a Decade: Variations by Sex, Race and Age* (Kalamazoo, Michigan: The Upjohn Institute, 1982).

6

Perceptions of Threat to Employment

Introduction

We are concerned here with perceptions of threat to the employment of women.[1] We ask the question, what developments, attitudes, structures, conditions, and arrangements give cause to women to be apprehensive about the security of their employment? In the chapter that follows we will examine the ways in which women have responded to the perceived threats to their employment.

In the past thirty years or so the number of women in employment and in search of employment increased almost four times – from 1,191,000 in 1953 to 4,299,000 in 1985. By contrast, the number of men in employment and seeking employment increased only 72 per cent over the same period. The main explanation for this difference will be found in the participation rates of men and women in 1953 and 1985: while most men of working age were in the labour force in 1953 (82.9 per cent of men 14 years of age and over), most women of working age were not (only 23.4 per cent of women 14 years of age and over were in the labour force). By 1985, the proportion of working-age women in paid employment increased to 55 per cent. In other words, in 1953 only one in four women of working age was in paid employment; in 1985 two in four were in paid employment. The information in Table 6.1 reveals the magnitude of increase and the extent to which the increase has changed the composition of Canada's labour force.

The substantially greater increase in the numbers of women than in the numbers of men is reflected in the composition of the labour force: in 1953 the labour market was dominated by men – the ratio was four to one; by 1973 the ratio changed to two to one; and by 1985 it

Table 6.1
Male/Female Composition of the Labour Force, Selected Years, 1953-85

Year	Total Labour Force ('000s) No.	Per cent Increase	Women No.	Per cent Increase	Men No.	Per cent Increase	Per cent of Total Labour Force Men	Women
1953	5,397		1,191		4,206		77.9	22.1
1963	6,748	25.0	1,870	57.0	4,879	16.0	72.3	27.7
1973	9,279	37.5	3,152	68.6	6,127	25.6	66.0	34.0
1985	12,725	37.1	5,490	74.2	7,235	18.1	56.9	43.1
Increase 1953-85 and 1963-85								
1953-85	7,328	135.8	4,299	361.0	3,029	72.0	–	–
1963-85	5,977	88.6	3,620	193.6	2,356	48.8	–	–

SOURCE: Statistics Canada, *The Labour Force*, Cat. no. 71-001.

reached 1.3 to one. This is a dramatic change in the composition of the labour force within the relatively brief period of three decades.

The variables that accounted for the increase in participation rates of women over the indicated period continue in effect, and some of them, such as postponement of marriage, postponement and control in the bearing of children, and more education suggest that the increase will continue. In addition, increasing numbers of women are entering professional and managerial occupations, which for the most part are lifetime career employments. These developments, and the employment opportunities associated with new technologies and technology processes, such as programmers, analysts, and researchers, will increase the proportion of women in the labour force to equal and perhaps exceed that of men by the end of the 1990s. In fact, this may happen sooner if the trend to early retirement by men in effect at present continues and becomes more widespread.

An examination of the employment of women over time will establish three significant developments: one is that total employment increased continuously in the past forty years. In only one year, 1982, did employment actually decrease. This is important when considered in the context of the employment implications of modern technology. At least half of that forty-year period is coincidental with the introduction and increasing use of computers, word processors, and other microelectronic instruments and processes. The second development highlighted in Table 6.1 is that the proportion of women in the labour force increased sharply in the past two decades, from 28 per cent of the total labour force in 1963 to 43 per cent in 1985. And the third development, which will be examined below, concerns the areas of activity in which women are employed. Even though women remain predominantly in traditional "female" employments, such as secretarial and clerical, sales and service, increasing numbers are now found in professional, administrative, and managerial employments. Since the participation of women in the labour force varies directly with levels of education, it can reasonably be expected that as more women finish high school and earn college and university degrees, more of them will enter the job market and more will remain in market employment longer.

The relationship between levels of education and participation rates is shown in the following statistics for 1985 (Table 6.2). Evidently, the higher the level of education, the more likely the person will enter into market employment and the more likely the person will remain in employment longer than those with less education. On the average, more than eight out of ten women with university degrees are in employment, compared with only four out of ten women with less than Grade Nine education. Also significant is the relationship between levels of education and age-related withdrawal from the labour market: participation by women in the 45-64 age group drops much more sharply among those with high school and some post-secondary education than among those with university degrees.

Table 6.2
Labour Force Participation of Women by Level of Education and Age, Canada, 1986

Age	Less than Grade Nine	Some High School	Some Post-Sec. Ed.	University Degree
15-24	35.4	62.6	66.8	84.1
25-44	46.7	66.9	75.4	83.8
45-64	32.9	49.9	59.1	71.4

SOURCE: Statistics Canada, *Canadian Social Trends*, Cat. no. 11-008E, Spring, 1987, p. 30.

Perceived Threats to Employment

Notwithstanding the evidence of continuous increase in employment of women over a period of more than three decades, agitation about possible negative employment has not abated. We explore below a number of possible explanations for the persistence of perceptions of threat to employment.

Technology has always been viewed as a threat to employment, despite the evidence that it creates employment: the capacity of new instruments, products, and processes to perform work functions performed by people, and to produce at a faster rate than people can, has led to the inevitable conclusion that technology is a threat to employment. In addition, there is the related perception that the amount of work to be done and the amount of output of goods and services to be produced are relatively fixed, while the technology is highly pervasive in its application to the production of goods and services. When one combines these three elements – capacity to produce wide-ranging goods and services, capacity to produce at increasingly faster rates, and a relatively fixed output of goods and services – the conclusion of threat to employment is unequivocal.

We can identify seven sources of perceived threat to the employment of women, most of them interrelated:

1. *The increasing rate of unemployment among women.*
2. *The threat of technology displacement*, directly by computers and computer-related instruments, processes, and products, indirectly through changes in the organization of work, dictated by new technologies.
3. *The pervasiveness of new technologies*, i.e., the increasing application of new technologies to wide-ranging work activities commonly thought of as appropriate for people only.
4. *The perception that while efficiency increases, the volume of goods and services to be produced is relatively fixed.* This is often referred to as "the lump of labour theory." It is viewed as a serious threat, particularly in relation to increases in productivity.
5. *The common tendency to extrapolate from past trends and to generalize* about future developments from experiences in individual cases.
6. *The pyramid shape of the occupational structure.* Large numbers of women are employed within the most vulnerable lower levels, in a rigid and closed system.

7. *The subordinate employment positions of most women.*

1. THE INCREASING RATES OF UNEMPLOYMENT AMONG WOMEN

Until the late sixties, the unemployment rates of women were on the average consistently lower than the average rates of men (Table 6.3). During the 1950s and early 1960s the average unemployment rates of women were almost half as high as the average rates of men, but beginning about the mid-1960s they started to creep upward and closer to the rates of men, and by the late 1960s they exceeded the rates of men and remained higher through the entire decade of the 1970s and part of the 1980s. It is natural that such a trend should give women a cause for concern.

Why have the unemployment rates of women increased so rapidly and so much beginning in the late 1960s and early 1970s? Why have they remained so high? Among the many explanations,[2] two stand out as the most plausible; one is the *crowding hypothesis*, the other the increasing *attachment of women to the labour force* and employment. The crowding hypothesis explains the starting period of the upward trend, whereas the attachment hypothesis explains the persistence of the high rates.

The crowding hypothesis has its rationale in the thesis attributed to Barbara Bergmann,[3] which postulates that because women have relatively easy access to only a few occupations and employments, they tend to crowd into those whenever large numbers of them enter the labour force. As long as the participation rates of women remained relatively low and the annual increase of women in the labour force remained moderate, the crowding did not present a problem, particularly since demand was also increasing in the employments in which women were crowding. Beginning in the late 1960s the early 1970s, however, the participation rates of women increased sharply and the annual increase of women in the labour force rose more rapidly, while the range of occupations and employments into which women had relatively easy access remained almost the same and demand remained relatively stable. The result was increasing unemployment.

The attachment hypothesis postulates that increasing numbers of women have become attached to the labour force and to employment on a continuing basis, and whenever they become unemployed, for whatever reason, they declare themselves as unemployed. In the past it was common for women, particularly married women, to withdraw from the labour market whenever they became unemployed. In other words, they did not declare themselves unemployed and looking for work. By not declaring themselves unemployed and looking for work

Table 6.3

Unemployment Rates by Sex and Age, 1953-87

Year	Men Total	Men 14-24	Men 25+	Women Total	Women 14-24	Women 25+	Total Total	Total 14-24	Total 25+
1953	3.4	6.0	2.8	1.6	2.4	1.2	3.0	4.6	2.5
1954	5.2	8.8	4.3	2.6	3.9	1.8	4.6	7.0	3.9
1955	5.0	8.6	4.2	2.6	3.7	1.9	4.4	6.8	3.7
1956	3.9	6.9	3.3	1.9	2.8	1.4	3.4	5.3	2.9
1957	5.4	9.7	4.4	2.3	3.6	1.6	4.7	7.4	3.9
1958	8.2	14.5	6.8	3.6	5.6	2.6	7.1	11.1	5.9
1959	7.0	12.3	5.8	3.0	5.2	2.0	6.0	9.6	5.0
1960	8.2	14.2	6.8	3.6	6.3	2.4	7.0	11.1	5.8
1961	8.4	14.1	7.2	3.8	6.4	2.5	7.2	11.0	6.2
1962	6.9	12.1	5.8	3.3	5.6	2.2	6.0	9.5	5.0
1963	6.4	11.7	5.2	3.3	5.9	2.1	5.6	9.4	4.5
1964	5.4	9.9	4.3	3.1	5.3	2.0	4.7	8.0	3.7
1965	4.5	7.7	3.6	2.7	4.8	1.7	4.0	6.5	3.1
1966	3.3	6.3	2.6	3.4	4.8	2.7	3.4	5.6	2.6
1967	3.9	7.2	3.0	3.7	5.5	2.8	3.8	6.5	2.9
1968	4.6	8.7	3.5	4.4	6.5	3.3	4.5	7.7	3.4
1969	4.3	8.3	3.2	4.7	6.5	3.7	4.4	7.5	3.4
1970	5.6	11.2	4.1	5.8	8.6	4.4	5.7	10.0	4.2
1971	6.0	12.0	4.3	6.6	9.8	5.0	6.2	11.1	4.5
1972	5.8	11.9	4.1	7.0	9.6	5.7	6.2	10.9	4.6
1973	4.9	10.0	3.4	6.7	9.2	5.4	5.5	9.6	4.1
1974	4.8	9.6	3.3	6.4	8.9	5.1	5.3	9.3	3.9
1975	6.2	12.5	4.3	8.1	11.4	6.5	6.9	12.0	5.0
1976	6.3	13.2	4.2	8.4	12.1	6.6	7.1	12.7	5.1
1977	7.3	14.9	4.9	9.4	13.8	7.4	8.1	14.4	5.8
1978	7.5	15.0	5.2	9.6	13.8	7.7	8.3	14.5	6.1
1979	6.6	13.2	4.5	8.8	12.7	7.0	7.4	12.9	5.4
1980	6.9	13.7	4.8	8.4	12.6	6.5	7.5	13.2	5.4
1981	7.0	14.1	4.8	8.3	12.3	6.7	7.5	13.2	5.6
1982	11.1	21.1	8.2	10.9	16.1	8.8	11.0	18.8	8.4
1983	12.1	22.4	9.2	11.6	17.0	9.6	11.9	19.9	9.4
1984	11.2	19.4	8.9	11.4	16.2	9.7	11.3	17.9	9.3
1985	10.3	18.2	8.3	10.7	14.6	9.4	10.5	16.5	8.7
1986	9.4	16.5	7.6	9.9	13.8	8.6	9.6	15.2	8.0
1987	8.5	14.8	7.0	9.4	12.5	8.4	8.9	13.7	7.6

SOURCES: Statistics Canada, *Historical Labour Force Statistics*, Cat. no. 71-201, 1973, 1983, 1974, 1984; *The Labour Force*, Cat. no. 71-001, December issues. (Annual averages.)

they were excluded from the labour market statistics – they were excluded from the supply-of-labour statistics and from the unemployment statistics. In more recent times, with the increasing commitment of women to employment on a continuous basis, they no longer withdraw from the labour market when they leave their jobs, even when they leave for maternity purposes.

Unemployment statistics showing the reasons unemployed women have given for leaving their last jobs (Table 6.4) can be interpreted to give credence to both the crowding and attachment hypotheses: only half of the unemployed women in 1987 had lost their jobs or were laid off. The other half were re-entrants and new entrants into the labour market looking for work. The crowding thesis suggests that large numbers of re-entrants and new entrants crowd already crowded employments; the attachment thesis explains the tendency of women to remain in the labour market when laid off and to return to the market looking for work on the completion of the tasks that caused them to quit their jobs.

Table 6.4
Unemployed Women by Reason for Leaving Last Job, 1987

Own illness	24,000
Personal responsibilities	40,000
Going to school	24,000
Lost job or laid off	272,000
Retired	4,000
Other reasons	110,000
Not worked in last 5 years	34,000
Never worked	25,000

SOURCE: Statistics Canada, *The Labour Force*, Cat. no. 71-001, December, 1987.

In addition to the crowding and attachment hypotheses, three other developments that explain the increase in unemployment rates among women are (1) the increasing entry by women into seasonal and cyclical employments, particularly in outdoor recreational activities, construction, transportation, manufacturing, and forestry; (2) the relatively high turnover rates common to women, particularly married women with young children who like to take summers off; and (3) the increasing tendency to stretch out the job search time after the loss of a job, which during the period of rising unemployment rates among women in the 1970s and 1980s was facilitated by improvements in unemployment insurance payments.[4]

2. THE THREAT OF TECHNOLOGY DISPLACEMENT

Joseph Schumpeter characterized technological change as the process of "destructive creation": it destroys jobs, products, and processes and it creates jobs, products, and processes.[5] It is possible that the production, distribution and use of the new technologies will create more jobs than they destroy. Nevertheless, concerns about displacement are legitimate. As long as the jobs created are different from those that are destroyed, the people who perform the jobs threatened by destruction have a just cause for concern, particularly in a system of job-training and relocation, such as the Canadian, which is highly imperfect and very ineffective.

Expressions of apprehension about the employment effects of the new technologies are often exaggerated by conceptions of production systems and networks in which human interventions are reduced to a minimum – systems and networks in which computers interact with computers in integrated computer-telecommunications office networks, computer assisted design and manufacturing, and integrated computer-telecommunications retail and financial services. If and when such systems are introduced and become operational, human interventions will indeed be reduced to a minimum. But then, when such an infrastructure comes into being the role of people generally will change as participants in production of goods and services and as income-earners. The concerns of today will probably differ from the concerns of that environment.

Nevertheless, it is well, perhaps, that we consider some of the characteristics of microelectronic technology that cause apprehensions. Two such characteristics have been identified: the "intelligent" functions of computers and the pervasiveness of the technology. The capacity of computers to perform "intelligent" functions, to think, represents a competitive challenge to the most specific attributes of the human factor. Unlike past technologies, which for the most part complemented and substituted some of the physical human capacity, the computer has the scientific potential to complement and substitute both physical and mental capacities.

Both substitution and complementarity can have negative short-run effects on employment: substitution is direct displacement, as in the case of computerized information banks that displace manual filing, search, and retrieval; complementarity, on the other hand, enables people to perform some work functions faster, which means output per person increases. This, too, can result in less employment, depending on the difference between the increase in output per person and the increase in demand for the output. With the aid of the computer an engineer can perform a number of functions much faster than with the slide rule and the calculator. The effect of that on the employment of engineers will depend on the demand for engineering services. Apprehensions about employment effects are founded on the expectation that demand may not increase at the rate of increase in computer efficiency, and new work activities may not be created fast enough to fill the emerging gap.

In relation to the substitution and complementarity to mental activities, the effects to date have been largely positive: for the most part the mental activities that have been substituted and those complemented have been activities bordering on mental drudgery – mathematical calculations, data manipulation, the storing (filing) of information, the retrieval and arrangement of data in different configurations, and so on. Accountants will attest to this, and so will engineers, economists, laboratory technicians, filing clerks, statisticians, and many others. What in effect has happened is that repetitive and monotonous mental activities have been eliminated from work processes or taken over by the computer systems, while other mental activities have been enhanced by the use of computers and computer-related instruments and products as surrogates.

It is the next phase of development in computer technology that gives cause for concern. The development of artificial intelligence challenges the highest attribute of the human person. The possibility that computers will be provided with mental capacities to seek out information, determine alternatives, choose from among alternatives, and make rational decisions signals significant change in the nature of human participation in work activities. The pervasiveness of computer technology extends this to about every activity in which people engage.

3. THE PERVASIVENESS OF COMPUTER TECHNOLOGIES

The pervasiveness of computer technology challenges the organization of production processes and the participation of people in them more than any other facet of the new technology. Unlike past technologies, which for the most part were specific to the processes for which they were designed, computer technology is multifaceted. As Colin Norman has noted, "No technology in history has such a broad range of potential applications."[6]

Three aspects of its pervasiveness give legitimacy to concerns:

one is the appropriateness of computer technology for many work activities that until now have been sheltered from technological changes. Most work activities known as "service" activities are in this category. They include general office work, work in financial institutions, insurance, and real estate, in retail and wholesale trade, in educational and health-care institutions, and in government services. Since appropriate technology did not exist for them, they became the major source of employment in the past three to four decades. Almost three-quarters of employed women are in such work. It should not be surprising, then, that women working in the services sector should be apprehensive about the security of their employment.

The second aspect concerns the increasing encroachment of the technology into work that has been thought to be totally in the human domain. This is the higher-level work involving decision-making functions in business, institutions, governments, and the professions. Women have long aspired to such employment, and for long they have been denied access to it in competition with men. Now they face the prospect of another competitor threatening their progress.

The third aspect of the technology is potentially the greatest threat to the employment of women: the evolution of integrated interactive computer telecommunications systems. When computers begin to interact with computers within enterprises and among enterprises, when the computers of bank customers begin to interact with the computers of banks and the computers of grocery stores interact with the computers of financial institutions in which their customers have their deposit accounts, scores of intermediary work activities will disappear. The human interventions that now exist in the process of completing transactive activities will no longer be necessary. When the point-of-sale systems of retail establishments are linked to the funds transfer systems of financial institutions, the interceptive work that now exists in the chain of transactive activities involved in a purchase (such as inventory adjustment, communication with suppliers for additional stock, processing of payment by credit card or cheque, credit and debit of respective accounts in financial institutions) will become redundant. Most of such interceptive work is now performed by women.

4. INCREASED EFFICIENCY AND THE VOLUME OF OUTPUT

The fourth source of concern is the perception that productivity is increasing faster than the volume of output. When the word processor doubles and triples the output of the typist and the volume of work doubles and triples, the job of the typist is safe; but when the volume of work remains unchanged or increases by less than the increase in productivity, an element of risk enters the employment environment.

There is a general perception that computers and computer-related technologies have very large and expanding production capacities. A state of perpetual excess capacity is perceived, in which case it becomes possible to increase the volume of goods and services without the employment of additional people.

The perception of threat is compounded by the expectation of slowdown in the rate of growth in the volume of goods and services to be produced. This increases the risk even more; for the problem is not one of increasing the volume of goods and services without hiring additional people; it is rather one of not increasing the volume, while productivity increases and the production capacity of technologies increases. The threat in such case extends to both the new entrants into the labour market looking for work and to the employed. When the amount of work to be done remains unchanged, while productivity and the number of people wanting work increases, then there is less work for each person who wants work. This is the "lump of labour theory."[7]

But this is not a realistic assessment of the existing and emerging environments. Although the production capacities of new technologies have been increasing and productivity has been increasing in activities to which computers and computer-related instruments, products, and processes have been applied, the volume of goods and services has been increasing as well, and so has the volume of work. The new technologies perform new work activities, produce new goods and services, and create new forms of employment. The record to date, after almost thirty years of experience with expanding productive capacities of new technologies, is that the volume of goods and services has increased substantially and so has total employment. An examination of the record over the past decade (1977-86), a period over which the introduction of new technologies has significantly accelerated, reveals that the volume of goods and services increased by 29 per cent, total employment increased by 21 per cent, and the employment of women increased by 38 per cent.

The seeming contradiction between the reality of displacement of workers by new technologies and the reality of increasing total employment in the economy at large is not a contradiction at all. It simply means that employment generally increased substantially more than the disemployment caused by new technologies and structural changes in the economy.

The direct effect of technology in established production processes is labour-saving; but the indirect effect is employment-creating.

This may appear contradictory, but it is not. Technology may displace labour from established processes, but it creates employment in the production of new goods and services, in the production and distribution of a larger output, and, of course, in the production, distribution, sales, and maintenance of the technology itself. In addition, the production of new goods and services and larger volumes of existing goods and services involve the production, processing, storage, and transportation of larger quantities of materials. This, too, creates employment. Finally, there is the significant employment effect of the increase in productivity and incomes. This is often forgotten because it comes through the expenditure of the increase in incomes and materializes over time. Yet, the increase in incomes is revealed in greater demand for goods and services, the production of which will create more employment.

Therefore, the technology-related increases in efficiency and output are not a threat to the employment of women. On the contrary, they are among the most important positive employment outcomes of technology.

5. THE TENDENCY TO EXTRAPOLATE AND GENERALIZE

A common caution to students in economics is to guard against the fallacy of composition: that which is true in an individual situation is not necessarily true generally. If an individual were to save most of his/her income, he/she will become relatively wealthy; if all the people were to save most of their incomes, all will become poor. The explanation for this is simple: if people were to save most of their incomes, demand for goods and services would fall, production will decrease, unemployment will increase, incomes will fall, savings will be used up, and people generally will become poor. Similarly, if a firm were to double its output with 20 per cent fewer workers, employment generally may increase, not decrease: the increase in productivity manifested in the doubling of output with fewer workers means the firm will have lower per-unit cost of production, which in turn means also the firm can decrease the price of the product, increase the wages and salaries of its employees, and increase the dividends of its shareholders. The decrease in product price means that people can buy more of the product with the same budget expenditure as before the decrease in price or buy the same quantity as before and something else with the same budget expenditure. In either case, total production will increase. Also, the increase in the wages and salaries of employees and dividends of shareholders will result in an increase in demand for goods and services. The outcome of both will be an increase in production and employment.

New technology, in the form of computers and computer-related instruments, products, and processes changes the structure of industries, including distribution and sales, organization of work, and education and training, which in turn dictates changes in the structure of occupations and employment. Experience indicates that changes in the structure of industry and the organization of work cause the elimination of some employment and skills, but at the same time the growth in the volume of work and the creation of new work activities cause new employment and skills. Often, what seems like a decrease in employment at one level or in one classification in the occupational structure is in fact a shift to another level and another classification: decrease in filing clerks is offset by an increase in data entry clerks; inventory clerks are offset by data control clerks; and the decrease in office machine operators is more than offset by the increase in computer operators. In addition, substantial employment is generated in the production, distribution, sales, demonstration, installation, and maintenance of the new technology.

A common weakness in the analysis of cause and effect relationships in economic matters is the tendency to limit the analysis to the first-order effects, that is, the immediate effects of a given change. Yet, the most significant effects, the final effects, are the second-order or even third-order effects over time. Analysis limited to the first-order effects is incomplete, and generalizations based on such analysis are usually wrong.

Case studies of individual processes are informative, but they do not in themselves constitute a sufficient basis for conclusions on the employment effects of computers and computer-related instruments, products, and processes in the enterprises where they are used, in related industries, or in the economy at large. The employment effects on the aggregate can be expected to be significantly different from the employment effects at the level at which a given instrument, product, or process is applied, regardless of whether that level is a stage of a process, a process, an industry, or a whole sector of the economy.

6. THE PYRAMID SHAPE OF THE OCCUPATIONAL STRUCTURE

Another source of apprehension emanates from the perception of the occupational structure as pyramid-shaped, with relatively large numbers of jobs at the base of the pyramid, progressively becoming fewer and fewer as one moves toward the top of the pyramid. The apprehension derives from the belief that most jobs at the higher levels of the pyramid are occupied by men, and through "old boys" networks and internal arrangements remain occupied by men. Women are largely excluded from upward progression. Therefore, as long as the structure remains pyramid-like and progression to the higher levels of the pyramid is limited, women will remain largely within the lower levels of the pyramid.

Information on where women are employed within the pyramid, and on the extent to which they have moved to the higher levels, provides just cause for apprehension: although increasing numbers of women have moved into the middle levels of the pyramid in the past decade or so and a few have moved to higher levels, the vast majority remain at the lower levels. Upward progression continues to be more difficult for women than for men, particularly when the progression involves the replacement of men. The problem does not appear as serious when the progression involves newly created positions.

This suggests the possibility that computer technology may, in fact, open opportunities for women to move into higher-level positions: information on changes in the configuration of the occupational structure over the past decade or so indicates that middle-level and upper middle-level employments have been increasing at higher rates than lower-level employments. As a result, the configuration of the occupational structure has been increasingly taking the form of a barrel. A change from a pyramid, which limits progression to vertical movement, to a barrel, which provides an opportunity for horizontal as well as vertical movement, will expand the range of opportunities for advancement.

Nevertheless, in the context of the pyramid-like occupational structure and the barriers that women have encountered to vertical progression within the structure, apprehension is fully justified. The increase in occupations and employments at the middle levels of the pyramid, which changes the configuration of the occupational structure, and the lowering of barriers to vertical and horizontal mobility may decrease somewhat the degree of apprehension, but, as long as women remain concentrated in employments threatened by technological change, the apprehension about employment security will remain. This suggests that the only long-term solution to the problem will be found in the decrease in employment concentration of women, which means opening opportunities to women over the entire occupational structure.

Opening of opportunities means giving access to employment experiences that will qualify them for promotions and admitting more women to educational and training programs dominated by men. Such initiatives, however, will be resisted by men, particularly in occupations and employments that experience limited growth in numbers. The admission of increasing numbers of women into programs of study and into employments where the numbers remain relatively constant means women will be displacing men. This will cause apprehension in the male population. Therefore, whether the configuration of the occupational structure remains a pyramid or becomes barrel-like, the movement of women into the higher levels of the structure in the absence of a general increase in the numbers of positions at the higher levels means the displacement of men. In this context, the threat is to men, not to women.

7. SUBORDINATE EMPLOYMENT

Most women hold subordinate employment positions and commonly report to men. In a hierarchical working environment, they are directly or indirectly supervised and evaluated by men. It is natural, then, that when work generally is being mechanized they should feel somewhat apprehensive and threatened. There exists this feeling that when choices are made between women and men, women are likely to be the first to go.

A related source of apprehension is the specific, non-specialized nature of work that many women perform. It is generally known that the more specific and non-specialized the work, such as telephone operator or typist, the more vulnerable the work is to technological displacement. Even the new technology-related employments to which many women have transferred in recent years, such as computer operator, data input clerk, and data control clerk, are specific and non-specialized and, consequently, highly vulnerable. The disappearance of the key-punch operator is a good example. As an occupation it lasted a mere twenty years. The specialized jobs, such as analysts and programmers, as well as the supervisory and managerial jobs have largely gone to men. This has heightened the sense of apprehension, since future employment security is commonly associated with managerial, professional, scientific, and technical jobs. To the extent that women remain largely in subordinated employment, even within the rapidly changing new technical infrastructure, their employment will continue to be vulnerable.

In this rather pessimistic scenario there is one encouraging development: unlike earlier technologies, which impacted directly on individual work processes and individual jobs, computer technology affects the organization of work. In many organizations the result is not so much the displacement of specific individuals from specific jobs as the introduction of new work activities, new channels of communication, new lines of authority, and a widespread shift of people. This is why there is still so much uncertainty about the actual effect on employment. What were thought to be job displacements are turning out to be job shifts.

In summary, most of the indicated threats to the employment of women have varying degrees of reality. Even where a reality of displacement at one level is offset by a reality of employment expansion at another level, the reality of threat is not necessarily negated. The fact of displacement is the reality. It depends, then, on one's perspective: from the standpoint of the employment people now have, computer technology presents varying degrees of threat to them; but in terms of employment generally, all signals indicate expansion. This is particularly the case in relation to many of the employments in which women engage: they appear to be most vulnerable to the new technologies, and at the same time they record the highest rates of increase in employment. Subordination remains a characteristic, but this does not appear to place employment at risk.

Notes

1. Parts of this chapter and the next are expanded versions of parts of a paper presented at a Colloquium on the Economic Status of Women in the Labour Market, convened by the Economic Council of Canada in Montreal, November, 1984. See Economic Council of Canada, *Towards Equity* (Ottawa, 1984), pp. 83-93.
2. For a detailed examination of the various explanations, see Marianne A. Ferber and Helen M. Lowry, "Women: The New Reserve Army of the Unemployed," in Blaxall and Reagan, eds., *Women and the Workplace*, pp. 213-32.
3. Bergmann, "The Effect on White Incomes of Discrimination in Employment."
4. Estimates of increases in unemployment as a result of increases in UI benefits range between 1.4 weeks and 2.0 weeks for Canada, and 0.4 weeks to 1.5 weeks for the U.S. See Royal Commission on the Economic Union and Development Prospects for Canada, *Report*, vol. 2, p. 607.
5. Schumpeter, *Capitalism, Socialism and Democracy.*
6. Colin Norman, *Microelectronics at Work: Productivity and Jobs in the World Economy* (Washington, D.C: Worldwatch Institute, Paper #39, October, 1980), p. 29.
7. Term used by Norman Bentwell in *Economic Aspects of Immigration* (New York: National Committee on Immigration, 1947), p. 27.

7

Responses to Threat

Introduction

We have examined the employment conditions that cause women to be apprehensive about the security of their employment and to believe that opportunities for advancement are limited. We will now examine the ways in which women have responded to the limitations of the existing employment structure.

Women are responding to discrimination in employment in ways common to discriminated groups in all societies throughout history: they are entering into professional and proprietorial occupations. Increasing numbers are becoming physicians, lawyers, accountants, personnel consultants, researchers, and equally increasing numbers are starting their own enterprises in various service and retail fields.

Such a response to employment discrimination is common in the sense that when groups in society find barriers to entry into certain employments or to advancement within enterprises, individual members of the groups seek out work in which they are independent of others in the evaluative process – occupations and employments in which success is determined by the impersonal forces of the marketplace and in which the individual is judged on demonstrated professional competence alone.

The evidence of such responses by women is overwhelming. In the United States, the number of women sole proprietors increased by 33 per cent between 1977 and 1983, compared to an increase of only 11 per cent in men proprietors. By 1983, over 26 per cent of all non-agricultural proprietorships in the U.S. were owned by women. In addition, the number of self-employed women has been rising continuously, exceeding substantially the rate of increase in self-employment by men.[1] In Canada, the number of women in self-employment increased from 191,000 in 1975 to 415,000 in 1986, or 117 per cent within the relatively brief period of one decade. [2] By contrast, the number of men in self-employment increased from 820,000 to 1,141,000, or by 39 per cent. Thus, although in 1986 the number of men outnumbered women in self-employment three to one, within the 1975-86 decade the number of self-employed women increased three times as fast as the number of men.

In the 1971-81 decade, the number of women in professional occupations increased three to nine times more than the increase in the total number of women in employment (Table 7.1). While the number of women in all occupations increased by 64 per cent, the number of women physicians and surgeons increased by 140 per cent (from 2,890 to 6,925), the number of lawyers and notaries increased by over 550 per cent (from 785 to 5,150), and the number of engineers by 534 per cent (from 1,220 to 7,740). These are remarkable changes, particularly in occupations that involve long periods of study and from which women were virtually excluded. They surely indicate a significant turning point in the education, training, and employment of women.

Increases of the same magnitude were recorded in other professional occupations. For example, the number of women systems analysts and computer programmers increased 438 per cent; the number of women economists increased 322 per cent; and the number of community college and vocational school instructors increased 359 per cent. By contrast, the numbers in traditional female occupations increased by less than the 64 per cent: typists and clerk-typists, only 21 per cent; elementary and secondary school teachers, 23 per cent; telephone operators, 13.5 per cent; and nursing assistants, aids, and orderlies, 40 per cent. The number of graduate nurses increased by 64.5 per cent, which is equal to the average for all occupations.[3] Clearly, a redistribution in the occupational structure of the labour force is in process.

The structural change is also evident in other specialized occupations, including some middle-income occupations. Indeed, the increases in some of these have been remarkable, reflecting perhaps the considerable agitation by women against discriminatory practices. Table 7.2 illustrates this: while the total number of women in employment increased by 64 per cent in the 1971-81 decade, the number in managerial and administrative positions increased by 247 per cent.

Some remarkable changes are in evidence in the managerial and administrative group of occupations: in sales and advertising, the number of women managers increased from 465 in 1971 to 12,610 in

Table 7.1

Women in Selected Professional Occupations in Canada, 1971-81

	1971	1981	Change, 1971-81	
All occupations	2,961,210	4,853,115	1,891,905	63.9%
Accountants, auditors, and other financial officers	15,655	43,470	27,815	177.7
Architects	115	420	305	352.2
Engineers	1,220	7,740	6,520	534.4
Lawyers and notaries	785	5,150	4,365	556.1
Law and jurisprudence*	615	4,220	3,605	586.2
Physicians and surgeons	2,890	6,925	4,035	139.6
Dentists	305	805	500	163.9
Veterinarians	70	550	480	685.7
Pharmacists	2,170	5,695	3,525	162.4

*Excluding Crown attorneys, judges, and others in the legal profession who are paid out of the public purse.

SOURCE: *Census of Canada*, 1981, Cat. no. 92-920, Vol. 1.

1981. Similarly, the number in financial management increased from a mere 630 in 1971 to 12,660 in 1981. The trends evidenced in these statistics have continued through to the present.[4]

These changes in the occupational structure of women at work reflect the onset of three realities: one is the relaxation of discriminatory practices in the admission of women into professional educational programs; the second is the evident decrease in resistance to the promotion of women to middle management positions; third, increasing numbers of women view employment the way men do, that is, as a lifetime activity. Such a perspective means that preparation for employment becomes purposeful, and employment itself is no longer accidental and interim, to be entered into temporarily while planning some other form of lifelong activity.

The purposeful preparation for lifelong employment is revealed in the nature of educational programs women have chosen in recent years. Increasing numbers are investing considerable capital, in the form of actual expenditures and forgone earnings, in degree programs

Table 7.2

Women in Selected Management Occupations in Canada, 1971-81

	1971	1981	Change, 1971-81	
Total Employment	2,961,210	4,853,115	1,891,905	63.9%
Managerial, administrative- related	58,305	202,300	143,995	247.0
Government officials and administrators	5,445	14,520	9,075	166.7
Other managers and administrators	23,200	104,440	81,240	350.1
Financial management	630	12,660	12,030	1,909.5
Personnel management	445	7,210	6,765	1,520.2
Sales and advertising management	465	12,610	12,145	2,611.8
Managers in trade establishments	1,315	6,185	4,870	370.3
Managers in community, business, and personal service industries	3,470	13,325	9,855	284.0

SOURCE: See Table 7. 1.

that provide qualifications for professional and managerial occupations (Table 7.3). In 1984 women earned 38 per cent of the Bachelor's
degrees and 36 per cent of the graduate degrees in commerce and business administration; 31 per cent of the undergraduate degrees and 24
per cent of the graduate degrees in economics; 42 per cent of the LL.B
degrees and 26 per cent of the graduate degrees in law; 38 per cent of
the M.D. degrees and 40 per cent of the graduate degrees in medicine;
26 per cent of the Bachelor's degrees and 16.5 per cent of the graduate degrees in computer science; 36 per cent of the undergraduate
degrees and 22 per cent of the graduate degrees in mathematics; and
73.6 per cent of the undergraduate degrees and 66 per cent of the graduate degrees in psychology. Overall, women earned 51.1 per cent of the
Bachelor's and first professional degrees in all disciplines, and 39.2
per cent of all graduate degrees. Only engineering appears to have resisted the trend, and considering the evidence from mathematics and
computer science, it cannot be argued women do not have the aptitude
for engineering science.

Table 7.3
Degrees Earned at Canadian Universities, Selected Disciplines, 1980 and 1984

Discipline	Bachelor's and First Professional Degrees				Master's and Doctoral Degrees			
	Total No.		Per cent Earned by Women		Total No.		Per cent Earned by Women	
	1980	1984	1980	1984	1980	1984	1980	1984
Commerce and Business Administration	8,698	11,985	27.9	38.2	1,918	2,036	21.1	35.9
Economics	2,444	3,433	24.6	30.8	439	418	17.5	24.4
Law	3,017	3,086	35.0	41.6	135	114	19.3	26.3
Architecture	559	475	20.4	29.7	81	54	21.0	16.7
Engineering	6,214	7,144	5.7	8.5	1,146	1,618	4.8	7.0
Medicine	2,232	2,129	33.6	37.8	334	460	41.6	40.3
Dentistry	491	487	16.7	23.2	10	19	0.0	21.0
Computer Science	1,128	2,708	24.8	25.8	177	255	16.4	16.5
Mathematics	1,580	1,731	36.6	35.9	194	253	20.6	22.1
Psychology	4,067	4,391	69.0	73.6	709	614	51.2	65.8
All disciplines	86,410	92,816	49.6	51.1	14,170	16,450	35.7	39.2

SOURCE: Statistics Canada, *Universities: Enrolment and Degrees*, Cat. no. 81-204.

These statistics show a remarkable change in the educational choices women have made in recent years, as well as the extent to which barriers to entry into educational programs have been lowered. In 1961, women constituted only 7 per cent of the university enrolment in commerce and business administration, 0.7 per cent of the enrolment in engineering and applied science, 9.8 per cent of enrolment in medicine, and 5.3 per cent of the enrolment in law. By 1971 the respective percentages increased to 13.9 per cent in business administration, 2.4 per cent in engineering, 20.3 per cent in medicine, and 14.9 per cent in law.[5] By 1984, women earned (as opposed to merely being enrolled in) 38.2 per cent of the degrees in business administration, 8.5 per cent of the degrees in engineering, 37.8 per cent of the degrees in medicine, and 41.6 per cent of the degrees in law! This reveals revolutionary change initiated and accomplished within a mere two decades.

It is notable that this remarkable accomplishment was achieved without legislative dictates and quotas. Evidently, all that was necessary was the relaxation in admissions into programs of study by universities. The rest was accomplished by merit. Women simply outperformed men and won out in competition.

The educational and occupational advances recorded by women over the past two to three decades are manifested also in their employment earnings: the number of women in the twenty highest-paid occupations quadrupled within the 1971-81 decade (Table 7.4). The ratio of men to women decreased in all twenty occupations, in some of them quite dramatically. In 1971, the ratio of male to female lawyers and notaries was 20:1; in 1981 it stood at 6:1. The ratio for physicians and surgeons shifted from 9:1 to 5:1; optometrists from 15:1 to 4:1; sales, advertising, and purchasing managers from 21:1 to 5:1; architects from 37:1 to 12:1; and so on.

But, notwithstanding the very significant increases in the numbers of women in professional and managerial positions, the distribution of women in the occupational pyramid remains highly distorted. Most women remain crowded in low-paying occupations (Table 7.5). The increasing entry by women in professional and managerial employments, and their increasing tenure in the employments they enter, will likely continue to increase their proportion in such employments, but it will take time before the distortions attain any degree of acceptable respectability.

Employment in the Emerging Economy

The employment record of the thirty-year-old computer age has been generally positive for women. Notwithstanding the early expectations of negative employment effects, activities in which women work have generally experienced employment increases. Most decreases are recorded in manufacturing and primary industries, where men, primarily, are employed. Certain office employments have recorded decreases as well, but these have been more than offset by increases in new office and office-related activities. For example, the employment of filing clerks decreased, but the employment of information input clerks increased; office equipment operators virtually disappeared, but their numbers are more than offset by computer and computer-related equipment operators. In addition, thousands of women have become involved in sales, demonstrations, and promotions of computers and

Table 7.4
Men and Women in the Twenty Highest-paid Occupations,
Canada, 1971 and 1981

	1971			1981		
	Men	Women	Ratio	Men	Women	Ratio
Directors general	39,445	1,480	27:1	36,320	2,535	14:1
Physicians and surgeons	25,345	2,810	9:1	30,255	6,505	5:1
Dentists	6,040	280	26:1	7,605	700	11:1
Judges and magistrates	1,195	70	17:1	1,770	200	9:1
Lawyers and notaries	15,340	770	20:1	26,530	4,890	6:1
Osteopaths and chiropractors	980	75	13:1	1,600	285	6:1
Optometrists	1,410	95	15:1	1,365	330	4:1
Sales, advertising, and purchasing managers	15,000	700	21:1	68,925	13,475	5:1
Veterinarians	1,615	70	23:1	2,180	510	4:1
Architects	3,835	105	37:1	5,730	490	12:1
Air pilots, navigators, flight engineers	4,120	20	206:1	7,560	240	32:1
University teachers	19,355	3,850	5:1	24,780	8,030	3:1
Members of legislative bodies	1,010	100	10:1	1,795	510	4:1
Administrators – teaching	22,750	5,690	4:1	25,965	7,970	3:1
Personnel and industrial management	3,585	420	9:1	17,920	6,905	3:1
Management occupations	37,155	11,630	3:1	189,860	59,930	3:1
Administrators in medicine and health	2,520	2,305	1.1:1	5,245	5,560	1:1.1
Government administrators	13,795	1,510	9:1	22,865	6,485	4:1
Air transport foremen	1,250	30	42:1	1,785	135	13:1
Physicists	725	40	18:1	1,165	70	17:1
Totals	216,470	32,050	7:1	481,220	125,755	4:1

SOURCE: Economic Council of Canada, *On the Mend*, 20th Annual Review (1983), Table 5-5.

Table 7.5

Top Ten Occupations in which Women Are Employed, 1981

Occupation	Number
1. Secretaries and stenographers	368,025
2. Bookeepers and accounting clerks	332,330
3. Sales	292,915
4. Tellers and cashiers	229,325
5. Waitresses and hostesses	200,710
6. Nursing	167,710
7. Elementary and kindergarten teachers	139,620
8. General office clerks	115,015
9. Typists and clerk typists	102,970
10. Janitors, charworkers, cleaners	96,735

SOURCE: *Census of Canada*, 1981, Cat. no. 92-920, Vol. 1.

computer-related instruments and processes, thousands more in research and development of products, systems, and applications, and many thousands of others are involved in various operational activities, such as programming, inputting information (data), information (data) control, computer operation, and scores of clerical activities. Furthermore, with the kinds of educational qualifications increasing numbers of women are gaining, it can be fully expected that their numbers will continue to increase in computer-related professional, managerial, and administrative employments.

Women in the Information Economy

All developments point to the emergence of a new economy – an information economy. This is a progressive extension to the agricultural, manufacturing, and service economies of the past. Researchers have concluded that increasing proportions of the national revenue will emanate from information work, and greater proportions of the labour force will be engaged in work related to the production, dissemination, and application of information. Marc Porat identified 179 information-related occupations, which he classified into five categories:[6]

Knowledge producers – scientific and technical workers (chemists, physicists, geologists, etc.), workers in mathematical sciences, social science specialists (economists, psychologists, sociologists, etc.), workers in engineering sciences, and "private information service providers" (lawyers and judges, architects, designers, physicians [50 per cent], dieticians, social workers, computer specialists, financial specialists, and such others).

Knowledge distributors – educators, public information disseminators (librarians, archivists, and curators), and communications workers (writers, artists, entertainers, editors and reporters, radio and TV announcers, photographers, public relations people).

Market search and co-ordination specialists – information gatherers (enumerators, interviewers, investigators, adjusters and appraisers, surveyors, and such other), search workers (buyers, insurance agents, stock brokers, sales representatives), planning and control workers (administrators, office managers, clerical supervisors, dispatchers, postmasters, production controllers, payroll clerks).

Information processors – non-electronic-based (secretaries, clerks, mail carriers, inspectors) and electronic-based (bank tellers, bookkeepers, cashiers, registered nurses [50 per cent], sales clerks [50 per cent], and typists).

Information machine workers – non-electronic machine operators (compositors and typesetters, engravers, pressmen), electronic machine operators (computer operators, peripheral system-related equipment operators, computer input workers), and telecommunications workers (telephone and telegraph operators, radio operators, television and radio repairs).

Most of these are projected to increase in numbers, and all of them together are projected to become an increasing proportion of the total labour force (see Figure 7.1). The implication for the employment of women in this is positive, since women constitute significant proportions in most of the occupations included in the five categories.

Employment Intensity of Information Services

Information services have certain characteristics that make their production, dissemination, and use expansive. This expansiveness, inevitably, makes employment in the information sector expansive. The characteristics are *paucity*, *perishability*, and *privacy*.

Although the stock of our general knowledge, particularly scientific knowledge, has expanded significantly over the past few decades, and the dissemination and use of knowledge has expanded rapidly,

Figure 7.1
Four-Sector Aggregation of the U.S. Work Force, 1860-1980
(using median estimates of information workers)

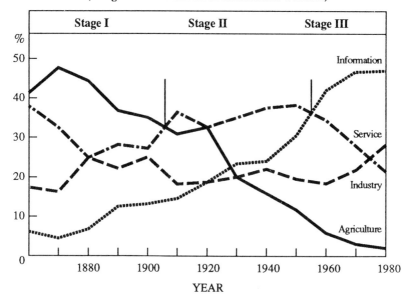

SOURCE: Marc Uri Porat, *The Information Economy: Definitions and Measurement* (Washington, D.C.: U.S. Department of Commerce, 1977), p. 121.

too, our knowledge of the variables that affect the human condition is still very limited. What we don't know exceeds by far that which we do know. Similarly, despite the significant improvements in the means of communication, the dissemination of information remains highly imperfect. Large segments of the population remain relatively uninformed even on matters that bear on their daily lives, such as employment opportunities, terms and conditions of employment, living costs in different parts of the country, and so on. If the people at large are to become effective participants in the marketplace in their capacities as consumers, producers, voters, and investors, they will need to be more knowledgeable and better informed. That means, of course, increasing allocations of human and capital resources to the processes for creating knowledge and disseminating information.

The second characteristic is common to much of the information that is consumed daily, which is provided in newspapers, magazines, radio and television programs, theatre productions, live concerts, and so on: it cannot be reused. Yesterday's radio and television schedule, like yesterday's weather forecast, is of only historical interest today. In other words, much of the information is perishable. And because it is perishable, it must be produced continuously. This has significant positive employment implications.

Continuous production is also dictated by the fact that much information is produced for private purposes. Although much is shared, much more is private. Large numbers of people are engaged in the search, production, analysis, and use of information for specific private and public purposes. Their information is not available for exchange. The secrecy, confidentiality, and intellectual property rights to information result in extensive duplication in information activities and in the output of information. The outcome of all this has been substantial employment creation in the information economy.

Thus, the pervasiveness of computer technology contains both positive and negative employment implications: while its capacity to perform wide-ranging work activities, including some activities requiring intelligence, is a serious threat to employment, its capacity to open new avenues to the creation of knowledge and to effective dissemination of information may expand employment. The emerging information economy suggests that the pervasiveness of computer technology may well bring about major changes in the structure of employment. Indications to date are that the structural changes tend to favour women more than men: employment activities in which women predominate have tended to expand more than those in which men predominate. Indeed, many activities dominated by men, such as those in the trades, have experienced significant decreases in employment.

Accommodations to Change

Changes in technology, increases in productivity, and changes in the structure of the Canadian economy are not new developments. The Canadian economy has recorded massive changes in the late forties, the fifties, and the sixties, which resulted in widespread displacements of industries and workers. Production processes in agriculture changed radically and employment in the agricultural sector decreased from 1.2 million in 1947 to 600,000 by the mid-1960s; the railways dieselized, and thereby caused a gradual reduction of employment by almost one-half within two decades; and hundreds of family stores gave way to the emerging department stores, chain stores, and super-markets. The displacement of workers that resulted from these structural and technological changes were accommodated successfully because in parallel with the contractions in employment were expansions of existing processes and products and the introduction of new processes and products. Not only were the displaced workers reabsorbed into the economy, but an additional 2.7 million workers were provided with employment between 1947 and 1967 – employment having increased from 4.7 million to 7.4 million. Clearly, the employment problems caused by technological and structural changes remain problems only when the economy fails to grow. Given adequate overall growth over time, displacements in individual processes, industries, and even sectors of the economy can be accommodated successfully.

A requisite to successful accommodation is, of course, the availability of effective retraining and relocation programs. This is particularly critical for advanced economies, where employment in most work activities is relatively specialized. It was relatively easy for Canada to accommodate successfully displaced agricultural workers into alternative employments in the late 1940s and 1950s without any retraining because expanding areas in the economy, such as construction, for example, did not require specialized skills. But with increasing specialization throughout the economy, it becomes more difficult to accommodate people in alternative employments without retraining. Successful accommodation is conditional on the existence of two elements: the availability and access to a range of alternative employment opportunities, and broad educational qualifications.

Women have had a legitimate reason to be apprehensive about technological and structural threats to their employment because the range of employment opportunities to which they have had access has been limited. Retraining for many women often meant retraining downward rather than upward in the occupational scale. Downward movements often meant movements into increasingly crowded markets, in which pay is relatively low and employment insecurity high. Queues become longer and longer, employers become increasingly more selective,[7] and job searchers shift from queue to queue, each lower than the other in the employment pyramid. This has not been an uncommon development, particularly for women who delayed entry into the labour market until after marriage and family formation, and for those who interrupted their employment for that purpose and then, after some years, sought to re-establish themselves within the pyramid.

Such women will continue to face the problem of downgrading, particularly those who find it difficult to remain up-to-date in their knowledge and skills and whose family responsibilities reduce the range of alternative opportunities for which they can compete. But for women at large the range of opportunities is growing, and their increasing educational qualifications in wide-ranging specializations are reducing their competitive disadvantage in the marketplace.

We have noted that the concentration of women into a few occupations and employments – secretarial and other office-support activities, retail activities, nursing and other para-professional health-care activities, and teaching – has been a common reality in all Western countries, regardless of differences in economic and social structures and governmental systems. This has been interpreted to suggest that perhaps women would not enter other occupations and employments even if opportunities were to be made available to them. A House of Commons Parliamentary Task Force on Employment Opportunities in the 1980s found shortages of machinists, electronic technicians, computer specialists, business and institutional managers, architectural and engineering technicians, telecommunications specialists, and, in a score of other occupations in computer and telecommunications activities.[8] The Task Force thought it paradoxical that these shortages had persisted over a relatively long period of excessive involuntary unemployment among young workers, both male and female.

While women stood crowded in low-level employments, vacancies existed in emerging areas of activity that promised security and advancement. Yet, there was no evidence that women were taking advantage of the opportunities. The Task Force made reference to "lack of training, negative attitudes, and social barriers."[9] Apparently, there were negative attitudes toward the so-called blue-collar occupations and social barriers toward occupations associated with and dominated by men. The report states: "Women are not being recruited actively enough or given enough chances to train in various trades ... apprenticeship programs must be opened up to accept more women. When this has been done ... supervisors have found that women can do the work as well as, or better than, men in the same trades."[10]

The problem is wider, of course, than the mere opening-up of apprenticeship programs to women: the attitudes of vocational guidance counsellors must become more gender-neutral; and employers must become more gender-neutral in the hiring and sponsorship of apprentices. Many apprenticeship programs require the prospective apprentice to find suitable employment with an employer who is a journeyman or who employs journeymen in the desired trade and who would be willing to act as sponsor, by entering into an apprenticeship agreement with the responsible government. Such conditions place women in front of a wall topped with barbed wire: they must not only scale the wall of employment discrimination, but they must also clear the wire. Apprentice sponsorship involves a multi-year commitment of supervised training, flexible time, and work relevant to the skill training. It involves also an expectation that the apprentice-employee will remain with the employer for some time after the apprenticeship program, so that the employer will receive a return to the investment in the employee. All this calls for an attitude toward women that is different from that which now prevails, particularly in relation to commitment to the work and the enterprise, length of employment, career development, and such other work-life relationships.

Attitudes change, of course, and we may well experience an influx of women into educational and training programs formerly regarded to be in the male domain. Not many years ago, few women were admitted into those bastions of male chauvinism, the medical schools, law schools, schools of business administration, and engineering schools; gradually, the fiction of gender exclusivity by association had to give way to the reality of the most qualified and admit increasing numbers of women. Now, almost half the students in medical and law schools are women, and the same proportion is approached by business schools in both their undergraduate and graduate programs. Even accounting programs, which long were associated with men (women occupying the lower-level positions of bookkeepers), are being invaded by increasing numbers of women. Only engineering schools have lagged in this, but indications are that there, too, the less able men will have to step aside for the more able women who wish to become engineers.

Nature of Education and Employment

A brief comment is necessary, perhaps, on the nature of educational qualifications that will provide access to a wider range of employment opportunities in the post-industrial society.[11] There is a view that the qualifications must contain a strong element of scientific, mathematical, and technical knowledge, including a satisfactory level of computer literacy.

There is no evidence to date of any need for such knowledge for employment, for security of employment, or for advancement in employment. A relatively small number of people are employed and are expected to be employed in activities that require esoteric technical knowledge. These are activities associated with the design, production, and maintenance of instruments, products, and the technological infrastructure. No technology, regardless how widespread in application, has been a major source of direct employment in design, production, and maintenance. The total number of technology-related jobs has always been a fraction of total employment.

In the instrumentation of work, the knowledge needed for work with the technology of the instruments, in their design, production, repair, and maintenance, is significantly different from the knowledge needed for work related to the use of the instruments in production. This applies as much to computers, word processors, video-display terminals, and printers as it applies to automobiles, sewing machines, typewriters, and airplanes. The idea that people have to have knowledge of the technology of computers and the language of computers to use computers is a fallacy perpetrated on the public by commercial greed. People need to be "computer literate" to use computers as much as they need to be "automobile literate" to drive cars. It is easier to learn what a computer can do and have it do what it can do than it is to learn how to drive a car efficiently.

Professor Joseph Weizenbaum of the Massachusetts Institute of Technology likened the commercial exaggerations to those of the pedlars of patent medicines. He said: "A new human malady has been invented, just as the makers of patent medicines in the past invented illnesses ... in order to create a market for their products, now it's computer literacy ... What a joke this would be if only it didn't victimize so many innocent bystanders."[12]

The victimization is particularly serious with children, who are distracted from the more serious business of learning, and with disadvantaged groups in society, including women, who are misled into the belief that knowledge of computers and the language of computers will lead to advancement in the occupational hierarchy and will provide them with employment security. Yet, as we have noted, in the history of technological change no technology has created any substantial amount of employment, and knowledge in the technology of machines and instruments has not been the most successful route for advancement in the employment hierarchy. Computer technology and the automated systems made possible by it will most likely generate less employment related to its design, production, repair, maintenance, and operation than other major technologies in the historical past.

The Challenge of Internal Barriers

All information on women in university programs and in employment indicates that entry barriers have been lowered significantly in the past two to three decades. The challenge that remains is to lower the barriers to occupational mobility within enterprises and organizations. Some progress in this is indicated in the statistics on women in managerial positions, but in the context of the total management and administrative positions in the economic and social infrastructure (including institutional and governmental), and in the context of the levels of managerial and administrative positions, the progress is modest.

The limited progression by women to the upper levels of the occupational and employment hierarchy can be attributed to the policies and practices that govern the operations of the internal labour markets of enterprises. The internal labour markets of large organizations are generally well structured, with fairly elaborate rules and practices relating to hirings, transfers, promotions, retirements, separations, and layoffs. But the rules and practices vary among occupational classifications and become increasingly arbitrary in the upper levels of the occupational structure. This is why the progress of women has been limited to the level of middle management. Up to that level progress is structured, with fairly well-defined rules and practices. Beyond that level the dominant variables become more subjective and arbitrary and the perspectives, values, and prejudices of the decision-makers are of greater importance.

This suggests that if women are to scale successfully the upper reaches of the occupational pyramid they might have to find ways to replace the elements of subjectivity and arbitrariness with rules, regulations, and procedures: rules on the hiring of people from the general market for positions above entry-level positions; regulations on intra-occupational relationships, transfers, promotions, and demotions; and procedures on the selection and assignment of people to activities that provide work experience deemed necessary for promotions. The relative absence of women from the ranks of senior management and from leading positions in professional occupations is generally attributed to their failure to bear any influence on the rules of the games being played within enterprises. Active participation in the making of the rules and in the interpretation and enforcement of those rules is a critical prerequisite to the introduction of fair play. When the makers of rules are biased, and the referees and umpires are biased, too, those who are discriminated against will not enjoy fair play regardless of how qualified and efficient they may be.

Affirmative Action

Affirmative action refers to initiatives designed to address the problem of inequity in the employment of women. It seeks affirmation of the right of women to equitable treatment and provides for the establishment of programs that would promote (1) the representation of women in desirable occupations and employments associated with and dominated by men, in some proportion of the total number of women with the requisite qualifications; (2) the introduction of programs and administrative measures designed to ensure that women have equal opportunity to men in educational and training programs; and (3) the introduction of procedures that would ensure fairness in assessments for horizontal and vertical progression within organizations, enterprises, institutions, and individual occupations. In short, affirmative action seeks to neutralize sex as a criterion in decisions on admission into educational and training programs and in decisions on employment, work assignments, assessments for promotion, and promotion. It seeks, in effect, to place women on an equal footing with men in competition for the limited places in desirable educational and training programs and for the relatively limited number of desirable employment positions in the economy and society at large.

Affirmative actions to combat discriminatory practices have been recommended by a number of investigative bodies during the past decade: the Parliamentary Task Force on Employment Opportunities for the 1980s (the Allmand Task Force, 1980)[13] recommended that "the Federal Government should encourage affirmative-action programs in the private sector and have a contract-compliance policy according to which it would only purchase from and contract with those employers who adhere to the human rights code and who have an affirmative action program as part of their corporate policy" (Recommendation No. 105). In addition, it declared that "Governments must show the way to the private sector by stepping up their own affirmative-action programs ... within their own departments and agencies, and in Crown corporations" (Recommendation No. 106).

The Royal Commission on Equality in Employment (the Abella Commission, 1984)[14] recommended mandatory affirmative action programs, both federal and provincial, to increase the representation of women where they are underrepresented because of discriminatory practices and to improve equality of employment opportunities for women. The emphasis is on affirmative action programs, policies, and procedures that will bring about *employment equity* for women. A Special Committee of the House of Commons on Visible Minorities (the Daudlin Committee, 1984)[15] recommended the establishment of voluntary affirmative action programs to overcome *systemic discrimination*, which is defined as an invisible and often unconscious form of discrimination embedded in the traditions and attitudes of society and built into the operational systems of enterprises and institutions. The recommendation for *voluntary* affirmative action is based on the premise that if sympathetic functionaries in the public services, in institutions, and in industry were to take the initiative and provide women with equal opportunities to employment and unimpeded progress within the employment structure on a free competitive basis, women will themselves negate whatever negative perceptions may exist about their capacities to function effectively in competitive and challenging work environments. But voluntarism is, by definition, an act of free will; and biased free wills have brought about the inequities that affirmative action programs seek to correct. Voluntarism will not bring about the changes in procedures and practices of institutions and enterprises. That is why the Royal Commission on Equality in Employment recommended a "massive policy response to systemic discrimination."[16]

Finally, the Royal Commission on the Economic Union and Development Prospects for Canada (the Macdonald Commission, 1985)[17] expressed general approval of the recommendations contained in the report of the Royal Commission on Equality in Employment, and made specific reference to actions that would require:

- Maintenance of existing equal-pay/equal-value policies
- Legislation that requires all employers covered by the Canada Labour Code, including federal Crown corporations, to take affirmative action
- Contract-compliance requirements for contractors working for the federal government
- Encouragement of provincial governments to follow suit.[18]

To ensure compliance, the Macdonald Commission recommended that the approaches be "firmly legislated rather that set out in guidelines," and that the Human Rights Commission be given the resources "so that it can strengthen its monitoring and enforcement activities."[19]

Regardless how "firmly legislated" and how vigorously the legislation is enforced, however, significant changes will not be effected without changes in perceptions of and attitudes toward women and without changes in evaluation and selection procedures within enterprises. The Soviet Union is a good laboratory on this. The Soviets engineered the most radical transformation of their society, with guaranteed employment, guaranteed incomes, support services for families and children, and equal opportunities to education, training, and employment, yet women remain disadvantaged in employment. In agriculture, "men work as accountants, section leaders, and farm managers" while women work as manual labourers;[20] in industrial occupations, women enjoy "opportunities for more satisfying and responsible work," but within the blue-collar industrial skills they tend to be "concentrated at the lower levels";[21] in the technical and professional occupations, such as engineering, the proportion of women exceeds substantially the proportions to be found in other industrial societies, but even though an engineering background is almost a prerequisite for management positions in industry, the management positions women hold tend to be in the technical and clerical categories that "do not involve executive leadership and authority."[22]

In the Soviet Union, medicine and education are two professions in which women predominate, yet in these occupations are found the most glaring examples of inequitable treatment. The 1975 statistics show that while women comprised 71 per cent of the total number of teachers and 80 per cent of the teachers in Grades One-Ten, they held only 31 per cent of the director (principal) positions of eight-year schools and 27 per cent of the director positions of secondary schools. The proportions "in teaching and administration at higher levels of the education system are lower still."[23] In medicine, "while men comprise 15 per cent of all medical personnel, they are 50 per cent of all chief physicians and executives of medical institutions .... In the overwhelming majority of cases, it is men who head departments, enterprises and administrative agencies."[24]

The Soviet record suggests that legislation proclaiming equal opportunity and employment equity must be accompanied by correspondingly appropriate initiatives that focus on changes in perceptions of women at work and in attitudes toward women with supervisory and managerial responsibilities.

Nevertheless, the Soviet record also suggests that changes in attitudes involve changes in generations, which means long periods of social and cultural transformation. In the meantime, it is necessary to establish the legal and regulatory framework, which manifests the common will. In Canada, the Employment Equity Act (1986) and the Federal Contractors' Program (1986) provide that framework. Even though their application is limited to employment in federal government departments and agencies, Crown corporations, federally regulated enterprises (e.g., banks and the transportation and communications industries), and suppliers of the federal government with contracts in excess of $200,000, they point the direction in which society is expected to move in its treatment of women in employment.

In conclusion, women have responded effectively to employment barriers and to threats on their employment by gaining qualifications and entering into expanding employment areas. In the process, women have challenged successfully the dominance by men of professional occupations and employments at the higher levels of the employment pyramid. Indications now are that women are better placed than men to take advantage of the emerging employment opportunities in the information economy. The legal framework now in effect at the federal level, when extended to the provincial, municipal, and private sectors, will increasingly transform that advantage into employment realities.

Notes

1. Dorothy Chansky, "The Rise of Women Entrepreneurs," *Economic Impact*, No. 50 (1985), pp. 42-45.
2. Statistics Canada, *The Labour Force*, Cat. no. 71-001, February, 1988, p. 93, Table 2.
3. All these statistics are from *Census of Canada*, 1981, Cat. no. 92-920, Vol. I.
4. See the special report by Statistics Canada, "Occupational Trends Among Women in Canada: 1976-1985," in *The Labour Force*, October, 1986, pp. 85-123.
5. Statistics Canada, *Historical Statistics of Canada*, second edition, 1983, pp. W430-38.
6. Marc U. Porat, *The Information Economy: Definition and Measurement* (Washington, D.C.: U.S. Department of Commerce, 1977); also see Fritz Machlup, *The Production and Distribution of Knowledge in the United States* (Princeton, N.J.: Princeton University Press, 1962).
7. Lester Thurow, *Generating Inequality* (New York: Basic Books, 1975).
8. Canada, House of Commons, Parliamentary Task Force on Employment Opportunities for the 1980s, *Work for Tomorrow: Employment Opportunities for the '80s* (Ottawa: Information Canada, 1981).
9. *Ibid.*, p. 5.
10. *Ibid.*, p. 76.
11. Daniel Bell, *The Coming of Post-Industrial Society* (New York:

Basic Books, 1973).

12. Quoted by Andrew Weiner in "Chip off the Old Block," *The Financial Post Magazine*, December 1, 1984, p. 40.
13. Parliamentary Task Force on Employment Opportunities for the 1980s, *Work for Tomorrow*.
14. Royal Commission on Equality in Employment, *Report* (Ottawa: Supply and Services Canada, 1984).
15. Canada, House of Commons, Special Commitee on Visible Minorities in Canadian Society, *Equality Now* (Ottawa: Queen's Printer, 1984).
16. Royal Commission on Equality in Employment, *Report*, p. 254.
17. Royal Commission on the Economic Union and Development Prospects for Canada, *Report*, three volumes (Ottawa: Supply and Services Canada, 1985).
18. *Ibid.*, vol. 2, pp. 642-43.
19. *Ibid.*, vol. 2, p. 643.
20. Gail Warshofsky Lapidus, *ibid.*, p. 128.
21. *Ibid.*
22. *Ibid.*, p. 129, quoting *Vestnik Statistiki*, 1 (January, 1975).
23. *Ibid.*
24. M. Sonin, *Literaturnaia Gazeta*, April 16, 1969, quoted by Lapidus, *ibid.*, p. 130.

8

Conclusion: Comments, Questions, and Policy Issues

1. In the formulation of policies and programs to achieve equality of opportunity for women in education and training, and in employment and promotions, it is well that the matter be approached from the standpoint of the consequences of unequal opportunities. Equal opportunity to equals should not be viewed as a favour to women, as it frequently appears to be, for in reality it is a favour to society and the economy at large. Unequal opportunity to equals is not only socially unfair but also economically inequitable, and it has negative effects on the rate of economic growth. It is socially unfair in the sense that people are discriminated against because they are women; it is economically inequitable because women are precluded from contributing to the full extent of their capacities and from enjoying the economic benefits commensurate with their productive capacities; and it is negative to the economy at large because potential output is forgone. In view of this, society has both a moral duty and an economic interest to ensure that all its human resources are given equal opportunity to demonstrate their productive capacities, and that all are allocated among productive activities in accordance with their demonstrated capacities.

2. Much has been done in the past two decades to reduce inequalities in employment and pay, and unequal access to desirable educational and training programs. The major force accounting for the progress has been the sustained offensive by women's groups against established discriminatory practices, re-enforced by the Charter of Rights and Freedoms and the pronouncements of investigative bodies, such as the House of Commons Special Committee on Visible

Minorities, the Parliamentary Task Force on Employment Opportunities for the 1980s, the Royal Commission on Equality in Employment, and the Royal Commission on the Economic Union and Development Prospects for Canada. Much remains to be done, of course, especially in relation to appointments and promotions to high-level positions, which continue to be occupied disproportionately by men.

3. The failure of women to advance into high-level employment positions is often explained on the ground that women are different than men in character, in temperament, in self-esteem, in language and gestures, and in interpersonal orientations.[1] Being different is not necessarily negative in itself, but it has negative consequences when women seek to enter working environments designed to accommodate the characters, attitudes, and values of the men who work in them. In this context, the question arises as to who should change: should men change to accommodate the characteristics of women or should women change to accommodate the male environment? One is tempted to say neither; yet, can organizations function efficiently when their high-level officers differ significantly in character, in temperament, and in interpersonal orientations? The evidence on this is too sporadic for a definitive answer. We will have to await the admittance of more women into the executive suites.

4. The most notable progress toward equal opportunity for women during the past two decades has been recorded in admissions into the programs of post-secondary institutions. No other enterprise in the Canadian economy and society has applied the equity principle as fully and unequivocally as have colleges and universities. The numbers of women in medicine, law, accounting, business administration attest to this. The historical record will show that it was not easy to change the perception of women within the male establishment in those occupations. But the change was initiated in the 1960s and accelerated when academic merit became the main criterion in admission decisions.

5. The employment record indicates that most women are concentrated into five traditional female employments: nursing and other health-care related para-professional occupations; teaching; secretarial/clerical; retail trade; and general services.

6. The concentration of women into relatively few occupational groups is usually explained as being the result of the limited range of employments to which women have had relatively easy access. When women thought of preparation for employment outside the household economy, those parts of the service sector were the only expanding areas into which they could enter with relative ease. Furthermore,

the alternative forms of employment for the levels of education most women possessed were relatively low on the social and economic scale. Therefore, efforts to bring about desegregation should not seek to cause women not to enter the traditional female employments, many of which, after all, are highly respectable; they should rather seek change in the classification of occupations and employments and in the ordering of occupations within the employment structure.

7. In addition to the easy access thesis, another plausible explanation for the concentration of women in the indicated employments will be found in their characteristics. Most of the traditional women's jobs are least in conflict with the traditional roles of women in family and society. The most important of these characteristics are: (1) flexible hours of work, (2) relative independence, (3) suitable work periods during day/night, (4) transferability of work experience, and (5) degree of investment in education and training required.

8. The policy approach to the problem of occupational segregation should begin with the recognition that segregation is *institutionalized*, which means that in many employment situations the role of women is instinctively perceived to be "different" from that of men: it is perceived as a subordinate role; a role not of leadership; a responsive role; a role of employment under direction. In this context, efforts at change must focus on change in perceptions of women at work and on the attributions to them of employment characteristics based on qualifications and experience without discounts for being women.

9. The institutionalization of employment segregation is reflected at three levels of the employment process: (1) *the classification of occupations*, whereby the occupations and employments traditionally associated with women carry lower classifications than comparable work activities performed by men; (2) *the organization of work*, whereby women are placed in subordinate work relationships often under the direction of or accounting to men; and (3) *the allocation of work responsibilities*, whereby women are denied responsibilities that will provide them with the nature and range of work experience regarded necessary for mobility up the managerial hierarchy.

10. The aspect of institutionalization responsible for much of the disaffection and exploitation of women in employment will be found in the classification of occupations and employments. Classifications determine who reports to whom, which establishes the rankings within the employment structure, and the relative values of the work performed at each classification. Change the classifications and the entire employment structure will change, concentration will disperse, and the ordering of relative values will change. Consider, for exam-

ple, the secretarial/clerical classification, in which 30 per cent of all women in the labour force were employed in 1987. The classification is extremely wide-ranging in the nature of activities performed, from the low-level junior clerk to the high-level administrative, executive, and personal secretaries. Many of these secretaries perform tasks and bear responsibilities that exceed by far the tasks and responsibilities of many managers. Yet, they remain segregated into the secretarial classification. Any effort at reclassification, and the bestowal of titles and values that represent more accurately the tasks women perform and the responsibilities they bear, will contribute significantly toward the evolution of an employment structure more representative of the structure of work actually performed.

11. The Employment Equity Act (1986) may well provide the needed impetus for desegregation. But legislation cannot establish an *ethic* of equal opportunity. Standards of ethical behaviour are set by society and enforced by social expectations. Therefore, two developments must follow: first, the law must be enforced vigorously and consistently; second, the enforcement process must evolve new standards of behaviour – it must be educative. The enforcement agency (the Canadian Human Rights Commission or some alternative Employment Equity Commission) should become a repository of cases detailing the employment experiences of women and those of employers in their efforts to desegregate employment and integrate women at all levels of the organizational structure.

12. The Employment Equity Act (1986) should be viewed as the first step in the process of desegregation. It should be followed soon with legislation applicable to the economy and society at large – to all enterprises (commercial, industrial, institutional) regardless of size.

13. The purpose of the Employment Equity Act and the Contractors' Program is not to prohibit; it is rather to evolve a change from employment practices deemed inequitable. Changing long-established practices that have come to be regarded as acceptable and fair can take a long time. Therefore, it is imperative that time periods be specified over which various aspects of employment equity are achieved. Without goals and timetables, the process may well be frustrated.

14. The achievement of employment equity will involve costs, which under the Contractors' Program will probably be reflected in the prices charged the government by contractors and in other programs in the prices charged consumers. Society should be prepared to bear the cost for the rectification of injustices perpetrated on women workers with impunity. The costs should be viewed as partial repayment for the exploitation of women in employment.

15. In the search for policies that will facilitate equal opportunity for women, the first would be to isolate the *variables that impede equal opportunity*. The most widely recognized impediment is the widespread belief that upon entry into employment women look at potential opportunities with a short-term perspective – an interim venture to be followed by marriage and children. Women differ in their responses to the challenges of employment, marriage, and family formation: some are intent on carrying on with all three simultaneously and continuously; others enter into employment on a temporary basis intending to withdraw upon marriage or upon the commencement of family and to remain out indefinitely; and still others enter employment and look at opportunities with long-term perspective even though marriage and family may dictate discontinuities in employment. The issue of equal opportunity arises in relation to all three categories: notwithstanding the intentions upon entry into employment, the experiences of employers indicate considerable uncertainty about the ultimate decisions. It would appear that with many women, independent decisions last only as long as they themselves remain independent of husbands and children. Thereafter their decisions are influenced by the family circumstances in which they find themselves. The uncertainty is a constraint on employer decisions to invest in women, but turnover rates among men suggest uncertainty in relation to them, too.

16. Efforts to achieve employment equity within a reasonable period of time will be frustrated without alternative systems of testing for potential to perform efficiently various ranges of work functions at different levels of the work pyramid. An examination of the work people do will establish that aside from those engaged in professional, para-professional, and craft work, the work functions performed by most people are only remotely related to their academic credentials, if at all. Academic credentials are good indicators of potential; but, after entry, the work undertaken becomes progressively a function of job experience. In view of this, it is imperative to the effective application of employment equity programs that systems of testing for work potential at different levels of employment be evolved.

17. Most discussions on the implementation of employment equity, affirmative action, and contractors' programs approach the matter from the standpoint of employment expansion – hiring, promotions, transfers. Some research should be undertaken on the question of employment equity initiatives in periods of employment contraction. In the absence of plans outlining processes and procedures in effecting employment contraction, there is danger of undoing over a brief pe-

riod of contraction all of the employment equity achieved over a long period of expansion.

18. The available evidence suggests that women remain in continuous employment over increasingly longer periods than in the recent past. This in turn is becoming reflected in the educational and training programs that greater numbers of women are choosing to pursue. These programs presuppose long-term career planning, and are not the *ad hoc* short-term programs commonly chosen in the past. In other words, for most young women it is no longer a question of two or three years of post-schooling work and then marriage and family; it is rather four or five years of work, marriage and work, family and work. This means that the changes are in family relationships, since work is becoming a continuing commitment. This is an important change, since the perception of women as short-term workers has often been held to be one of the considerations in not training them for managerial positions.

19. To the extent that women have been constrained in their choices of employment by their traditional dual responsibilities, it is incumbent on society to address the constraining variables. For example, to the extent that the pressure of young children is a constraining variable, day-care facilities and programs would be the accommodating response.

20. Close to 50 per cent of women with children under 14 years of age are in the labour force and indications are that the proportion will continue to rise. This suggests the need for a comprehensive system of assistance that would incorporate (a) maternity leave standards, (b) employment security for women on maternity leave, (c) income maintenance during periods of leave, and (d) child-care facilities and programs. Effective implementation of a comprehensive system of this nature depends on the involvement of all parties to the process, namely, employers, workers, and all three levels of government – federal and provincial governments in the setting of standards and financial participation; employers and employees with partial contributions to the financing of the system and in the establishment of child-care facilities; and municipalities in the supervision of child-care facilities and programs.

21. The organization and financing of day-care facilities and programs should be conceived in terms of an extension of the school system and should be open to all children regardless of whether their mothers are employed in the commercial or in the household economy. Considering that our society depends to a very significant degree on volunteer services, women employed in the household economy may

be able to allocate more time to volunteer activities if their children are to have access to day-care programs over varying periods of time during the day. Furthermore, while all mothers may be good mothers, all mothers are not necessarily good at raising children. There is no conceivable reason that schooling should begin at age five.

22. It is generally expected that by the end of this century, computer/telecommunications networks will increasingly integrate the household and market economies. Integration will facilitate participation in the market economy from home. The resultant changes in the organization and location of work, however, do not necessarily mean capacity on the part of women to participate effectively in all the activities of the household economy and in the market economy. Mothers of young children working from home will need the services of day-care as much as those working away from home. The rationale for day-care for all children remains valid.

Selected Bibliography

Aaron, H., and C. Lousy. *The Comparable Worth Controversy*. Washington, D.C.: The Brookings Institution, 1986.

Armstrong, Pat, and Hugh Armstrong. *A Working Majority: What Women Must Do for Pay*. Ottawa: Canadian Advisory Council on the Status of Women, 1983.

Ashenfelter, Orley, and R. Layard, eds. *Handbook of Labor Economics*. Amsterdam: North-Holland Press, 1987.

Ashenfelter, Orley, and Albert Rees, eds. *Discrimination in Labor Markets*. Princeton, N.J.: Princeton University Press, 1973.

Barro, Robert J. *Rules Versus Discretion*. Working Paper No. 1473. Cambridge, Mass.: National Bureau of Economic Research, September, 1984.

Becker, G. *The Economics of Discrimination*. Second edition. Chicago: University of Chicago Press, 1971.

_____. *Human Capital*. Chicago: University of Chicago Press, 1975.

_____. *A Treatise on the Family*. Cambridge, Mass.: Harvard University Press, 1981.

Bell, Daniel. *The Coming of Post-Industrial Society*. New York: Basic Books, 1973.

Beller, Andrea H. "The Impact of Equal Employment Laws on the Male/Female Earnings Differential," in C.B. Lloyd *et al.*, eds., *Women in the Labor Market* (New York: Columbia University Press, 1979).

Best, Fred. *Work Sharing: Issues, Policy Options and Prospects*. Kalamazoo, Mich.: The Upjohn Institute, 1981.

Blau, Francine D. "Discrimination Against Women: Theory and Evidence," in W.A. Darity, Jr., ed., *Labor Economics: Modern Views* (Boston: Kluwer-Nijhoff, 1984).

Blaxall, Martha, and Barbara Reagan, eds. *Women and the Workplace.* Chicago: University of Chicago Press, 1976.

Block, W., and M. Walker, eds. *Discrimination, Affirmative Action and Equal Opportunity.* Vancouver: The Fraser Institute, 1982.

Block, W., and M. Walker. *Focus on Employment Equity: A Critique of the Abella Royal Commission Report.* Vancouver: The Fraser Institute, 1985.

Boothby, Daniel. *Women Re-entering the Labour Force and Training Programs: Evidence from Canada.* Ottawa: Economic Council of Canada, 1985.

Boulet, J.A., and L. Lavallée. *The Changing Economic Status of Women.* Ottawa: Economic Council of Canada, 1984.

Boulet, Jac-André, and Laval Lavallée. *Women and the Labour Market: An Analytical Framework.* Discussion Paper No. 207. Ottawa: Economic Council of Canada, 1981.

Bowen, W.G., and T.A. Finegan. *The Economics of Labor Force Participation.* Princeton, N.J.: Princeton University Press, 1969.

Boyd, Monica. "Occupational Segregation: A Review," in *Sexual Equality in the Workplace* (Ottawa: Women's Bureau, Labour Canada, 1982).

_____. *Canadian Attitudes Toward Women: Thirty Years of Change, 1954-1984.* Ottawa: Women's Bureau, Labour Canada, 1984.

Breton, Albert. *Marriage, Population and the Labour Force Participation of Women.* Ottawa: Economic Council of Canada, 1984.

Cain, Glen G. *Married Women in the Labor Force.* Chicago: University of Chicago Press, 1966.

_____. *The Welfare Economic Policies Towards Women.* Madison, Wisc.: Institute for Research on Poverty, 1983.

_____. *The Economic Analysis of Labor Market Discrimination: A Survey.* Madison, Wisc.: Institute for Research on Poverty, 1984.

Canada, Department of Employment and Immigration. *Labour Market Developments in the 1980s.* Ottawa: Information Canada, 1981.

Canada, House of Commons, Task Force on Employment Opportunities in the '80s. *Work for Tomorrow: Employment Opportunities for the '80s.* Ottawa: Information Canada, 1981.

Canada, House of Commons, Special Committee on Visible Minorities in Canadian Society. *Equality Now.* Ottawa: Queen's Printer,

1984.

Canada, Labour Canada, Women's Bureau. *Sex Discrimination in the Canadian Labour Market: Theories, Data and Evidence.* Ottawa, 1981.

Canada, Royal Commission on Equality in Employment. *Report.* Ottawa: Supply and Services Canada, 1984.

Canada, Royal Commission on the Economic Union and Development Prospects for Canada *Report.* Vols. One and Two. Toronto: University of Toronto Press, 1985.

Canada, Statistics Canada. *Earnings of Men and Women 1981 and 1982.* Cat. no. 13-577. Ottawa, 1985.

Canada, Statistics Canada. *A Statistical Portrait of Canadian Higher Education: From the 1970s to the 1980s.* Ottawa, 1983.

Cetron, Marvin. *Jobs of the Future.* New York: McGraw-Hill, 1984.

Cook, G., ed. *Opportunity for Choice: A Goal for Women in Canada.* Ottawa: Statistics Canada, 1976.

David-McNeil, Jeannine. "The Changing Economic Status of the Female Labour Force," in *Towards Equity* (Ottawa: Economic Council of Canada, 1985), pp. 1-8.

Deaux, Kay, and J.C. Ullman. *Women of Steel: Female Blue-Collar Workers in the Basic Steel Industry.* New York: Praeger, 1983.

Doeringer, P., and M. Piore. *Internal Labor Markets and Manpower Analysis.* Lexington, Mass.: D.C. Heath, 1971.

Economic Council of Canada. *People and Jobs: A Study of the Canadian Labour Market.* Ottawa: Supply and Services Canada, 1978.

Economic Council of Canada. *In Short Supply: Jobs and Skills in the 1980s.* Ottawa: Supply and Services Canada, 1982.

Economic Council of Canada. *On the Mend.* Ottawa: Supply and Services Canada, 1983.

Economic Council of Canada. *Towards Equity.* Ottawa: Supply and Services Canada, 1984.

Economic Council of Canada. *Innovation and Jobs in Canada.* Ottawa: Supply and Services Canada, 1987.

Edwards, R., M. Reich, and D. Gordon, eds. *Labor Market Segmentations.* Lexington, Mass.: D.C. Heath, 1975.

Ehrenberg, Ronald G., and Robert A. Smith. *Comparable Worth in the Public Sector.* Working Paper No. 1471. Cambridge, Mass.: National Bureau of Economic Research, September, 1984.

Faulkner, W., and E. Arnold, eds. *Smothered by Invention: Technology in Women's Lives.* London: Pluto Press, 1985.

Fuchs, Victor R. "Recent Trends and Long-Run Prospects for Female Earnings," *American Economic Review: Papers and Proceed-*

ings (May, 1974), pp. 236-42.

_____. *His and Hers: Gender Differences in Work and Income, 1959-1979*. Cambridge, Mass.: National Bureau of Economic Research, 1984.

Gershuny, Jonathan. *After Industrial Society? The Emerging Self-Service Economy*. London: Macmillan, 1978.

Ginsburg, Helen. *Full Employment and Public Policy in the United States and Sweden*. Lexington, Mass.: Lexington Books, 1983.

Gotlieb, C.C., ed. *The Information Economy: Its Implication for Canada's Industrial Strategy*. Ottawa: The Royal Society of Canada, 1984.

Gunderson, M. "Discrimination, Equal Pay, and Equal Opportunities in the Labour Market," in Craig Riddell, ed., *Work and Pay: The Canadian Labour Market*, Study No. 17, Royal Commission on the Economic Union and Development Prospects for Canada (Toronto: University of Toronto Press, 1985).

_____. *The Male-Female Earnings Gap: A Current Assessment*. Toronto: Ontario Ministry of Labour, 1980.

Gunderson, M., and Frank Reid. *Sex Discrimination in the Canadian Labour Market: Theories, Data and Evidence*. Ottawa: Labour Canada, Women's Bureau, 1983.

Hammermesh, D., and A. Rees. *The Economics of Work and Pay*. New York: Harper and Row, 1984.

Hartmann, Heidi, ed. *Comparable Worth: New Directions for Research*. Washington, D.C.: National Academy Press, 1985.

Hunt, A. *Management Attitudes and Practices Towards Women at Work*. London: HMSO, 1975.

Hunt, H.A., and T.L. Hunt. *Clerical Employment and Technological Change*. Kalamazoo, Mich.: The Upjohn Institute, 1986.

Johnson, George, and Gary Solon. *Pay Differences Between Women's and Men's Jobs: The Empirical Foundations of Comparable Worth Legislation*. Working Paper No. 1472. Cambridge, Mass.: National Bureau of Economic Research, September, 1984.

Jones, Ethel B. *Determinants of Female Re-Entrant Employment*. Kalamazoo, Mich.: The Upjohn Institute, 1983.

Joseph, George. *Women at Work: The British Experience*. Oxford: Oxford University Press, 1983.

Killingsworth, Mark. *Labor Supply*. Cambridge: Harvard University Press, 1983.

_____. "The Economics of Comparable Worth: Analytical, Empirical and Policy Questions," in Heidi Hartmann, ed., *Comparable Worth: New Directions for Research* (Washington, D.C.: Na-

170 WOMEN AT WORK

tional Academy Press, 1985).

Kleinschrod, Walter A. *Critical Issues in Office Automation.* New York: McGraw-Hill, 1986.

Kreps, Juanita. *Sex in the Marketplace: American Women at Work.* Baltimore: Johns Hopkins University Press, 1971.

Kreps, Juanita, and Robert Clark. *Sex, Age and Work: The Changing Composition of the Labor Force.* Baltimore: Johns Hopkins University Press, 1975.

Livernash, E.R., ed. *Comparable Worth: Issues and Alternatives.* Washington, D.C.: Equal Opportunity Advisory Council, 1980.

Lloyd, C.B., *et al.,* eds. *Women in the Labor Market.* New York: Columbia University Press, 1979.

Lloyd, Cynthia B., and Beth Niemi. "Sex Differences in Labor Supply Elasticity: The Implications of Sectoral Shifts in Demand," *American Economic Review: Papers and Proceedings* (May, 1978), pp. 78-83.

Machlup, Fritz. *The Production and Distribution of Knowledge in the United States.* Princeton, N.J.: Princeton University Press, 1962.

Marstrand, Pauline, ed. *New Technology and the Future of Work and Skills.* London: Frances Pinter, 1984.

Melts, Noah, Frank Reid, and Gerald Swartz. *Work Sharing.* Toronto: University of Toronto Press, 1981.

Menzies, H. *Women and the Chip.* Ottawa: Institute for Research on Public Policy, 1981.

Oakley, A. *Housewife: High Value and Low Cost.* Hammondsworth: Penguin, 1976.

Organization for Economic Co-operation and Development. *Microelectronics, Robotics and Jobs.* Paris: OECD, 1982.

Paringer, Lynn. "Women and Absenteeism: Health or Economics?," *American Economic Review: Papers and Proceedings(May, 1983), pp. 123-27.*

Parnes, Herbert S. *Unemployment Experience of Individuals Over a Decade: Variations by Sex, Race and Age.* Kalamazoo, Mich.: The Upjohn Institute, 1982.

Paul, Betty Clayton. "Absences from Work Due to Illness," *The Labour Force,* Cat. no. 71-001 (Ottawa: Statistics Canada, March, 1984), pp. 91-100.

Pearson, Mary. *The Second Time Around: A Study of Women Returning to the Work Force.* Ottawa: Canadian Advisory Council on the Status of Women, 1979.

Peitchinis, Stephen G. *The Effect of Technological Changes on Educational and Skill Requirements of Industry.* Ottawa: Department of Industry, Trade and Commerce, 1978.

_____. *The Employment Implications of Computers and Telecommunications Technology*. Study no. 5412-4-5. Ottawa: Department of Communications, 1981.

_____. *Computer Technology and Employment: Retrospect and Prospect*. London: Macmillan, 1985.

_____. *Issues in Management-Labour Relations in the 1990s*. London: Macmillan, 1985.

Polachek, S. "Occupational Self-Selection in Human Capital Approach to Sex Differences in Occupational Structure," *Review of Economics and Statistics* (February, 1981), pp. 60-69.

Porat, Mark U. *The Information Economy: Definition and Measurement*. Washington, D.C.: U.S. Department of Commerce, 1977.

Remick, Helen, ed. *Comparable Worth and Wage Discrimination*. Philadelphia: Temple University Press, 1984.

Reskin, B.F. ed. *Sex Segregation in the Workplace: Trends, Explanations, and Remedies*. Washington, D.C.: National Academy Press, 1984.

Riddell, Craig W., ed. *Work and Pay: The Canadian Labour Market*. Study No. 17. Royal Commission on the Economic Union and Development Prospects for Canada. Toronto: University of Toronto Press, 1985.

Robb, Roberta Edgecombe. *Equal Pay for Work of Equal Value: Issues and Policies*. Ryerson Lectures in Economics, Lecture No. 22. Toronto: Ryerson Polytechnical Institute, 1986.

Rosen, S., ed. *Studies in Labor Markets*. Chicago: University of Chicago Press, 1981.

Ruffieux, Bernard. "New Technology and Women's Employment: Notes on a Debate," *Social Change and Technology in Europe*, Bulletin No. 5, Commission of the European Communities, Brussels, 1982.

Schultz, Theodore W., ed. *Economics of the Family: Marriage, Children, and Human Capital*. Chicago: University of Chicago Press, 1975.

Shaiken, Hurley. *Work Transformed: Automation and Labor in the Computer Age*. New York: Holt, Rinehart and Winston, 1984.

Smith, J.P., ed. *Female Labor Supply Theory and Estimation*. Princeton, N.J.: Princeton University Press, 1980.

Strassmann, Paul A. *Information Payoff: The Transformation of Work in the Electronic Age*. New York: The Free Press, 1985.

Swords-Isherwood, Nuala, *et al.* "Technical Change and Its Effect on Employment Opportunities for Women," in Pauline Marstrand, ed., *New Technology and the Future of Work and Skills* (London: Frances Pinter, 1984).

Thurow, Lester C. *Generating Inequality: Mechanisms of Distribution in the U.S. Economy.* New York: Basic Books, 1975.

Toffler, Alvin. *The Third Wave.* New York: Bantam Books, 1981.

Treiman, D.J., and H.I. Hartmann. *Women, Work, and Wages: Equal Pay for Jobs of Equal Value.* Washington, D.C.: National Academy Press, 1981.

Usher, Dan. *The Economic Prerequisites for Democracy.* London: Basil Blackwell, 1981.

Wallace, Joan. *Part-time Work in Canada: Report of the Commission of Inquiry into Part-time Work.* Ottawa: Labour Canada, 1983.

Werneke, Diane. *Microelectronics and Office Jobs: The Impact of the Chip on Women's Employment.* Geneva: ILO, 1983.

White, Julie. *Women and Part-Time Work.* Ottawa: Canadian Advisory Council on the Status of Women, 1983.

Wilkinson, F., ed. *The Dynamics of Labour Market Segmentation.* New York: Academic Press, 1984.

Index